European Computer Driving Licence®

Syllabus 1.5

Module AM4 - Spreadsheets

Advanced Level

Using Microsoft® Excel 2007

Release ECDL172v1

Published by:

> CiA Training Ltd
> Business & Innovation Centre
> Sunderland Enterprise Park
> Sunderland SR5 2TH
> United Kingdom

> Tel: +44 (0) 191 549 5002
> Fax: +44 (0) 191 549 9005

> E-mail: info@ciatraining.co.uk
> Web: www.ciatraining.co.uk

> **ISBN-13: 978-1-86005-596-6**

Important Note

This guide was written using *Windows Vista*. If using *Windows XP* some dialog boxes will look different, although the content is the same.

A screen resolution of 1024 x 768 was used. Working in a different screen resolution, or with an application window which is not maximised, will change the look of the *Office 2007* Ribbon.

The ribbon appearance is dynamic, it changes to fit the space available. The full ribbon may show a group containing several options, but if space is restricted it may show a single button that you need to click to see the same options, e.g.

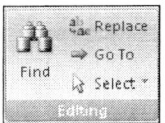

the **Editing** group may be replaced by the **Editing** button

---

First published 2007

Copyright © 2007 CiA Training Ltd

European Computer Driving Licence, ECDL, International Computer Driving Licence, ICDL, e-Citizen and related logos are trade marks of The European Computer Driving Licence Foundation Limited ("ECDL Foundation") in Ireland and other countries.

CiA Training Ltd is an entity independent of the ECDL Foundation and is not associated with ECDL Foundation in any manner. This courseware publication may be used to assist candidates to prepare for **ECDL/ICDL tests**. Neither ECDL Foundation nor **CiA Training Ltd** warrants that the use of this courseware publication will ensure passing of **ECDL/ICDL tests**. This courseware publication has been independently reviewed and approved by ECDL Foundation as complying with the following standard:

*Technical compliance with the learning objectives of **ECDL/ICDL AM4 Advanced Spreadsheets Syllabus Version 1.0**.*

Confirmation of this approval can be obtained by reviewing the Courseware Section of the website **www.ecdl.com**.

The material contained in this courseware publication has not been reviewed for technical accuracy and does not guarantee that candidates will pass **ECDL/ICDL tests**. Any and all assessment items and/or performance-based exercises contained in this courseware publication relate solely to this publication and do not constitute or imply certification by ECDL Foundation in respect of **ECDL/ICDL tests** or any other ECDL Foundation test.

For details on sitting **ECDL/ICDL tests** and other ECDL Foundation tests in your country, please contact your country's National ECDL/ICDL designated Licensee or visit ECDL Foundation's web site at www.ecdl.com.

Candidates using this courseware publication must be registered with the National Licensee, before undertaking **ECDL/ICDL tests**. Without a valid registration, **ECDL/ICDL tests** cannot be undertaken and no **ECDL/ICDL** certificate, nor any other form of

ECDL Foundation
Approved Courseware

recognition, can be given to a candidate. Registration should be undertaken with your country's National ECDL/ICDL designated Licensee at any Approved **ECDL/ICDL** Test Centre.

ECDL/ICDL AM4 Advanced Spreadsheets Syllabus Version 1.0 is the official syllabus of the **ECDL/ICDL** certification programme at the date of approval of this courseware publication.

Downloading the Data Files

The data associated with these exercises must be downloaded from our website. Go to: ***www.ciatraining.co.uk/data***. Follow the on screen instructions to download the appropriate data files.

By default, the data files will be downloaded to **Documents\CIA DATA FILES\Advanced ECDL\AM4 Excel 2007 Data** (Note: *Windows XP* downloads to a **My Documents** folder).

If you prefer, the data can be supplied on CD at an additional cost. Contact the Sales team at ***info@ciatraining.co.uk***.

Aims

To provide the student with an understanding of the more advanced concepts of spreadsheet models using Excel.

Objectives

After completing the guide the user will be able to:

- Create and maintain complex spreadsheets
- Manipulate charts
- Create and use Scenarios
- Create and use Templates
- Link cells, worksheets and workbooks
- Use complicated Functions of various types
- Use Data Tables and Databases
- Create and use simple Macros
- Use Auditing techniques to check for errors

Assessment of Knowledge

At the end of this guide is a section called the **Record of Achievement Matrix**. Before the guide is started it is recommended that the user complete the matrix to measure the level of current knowledge.

Tick boxes are provided for each feature. **1** is for no knowledge, **2** some knowledge and **3** is for competent.

After working through a section, complete the **Record of Achievement Matrix** for that section and only when competent in all areas move on to the next section.

Contents

Section 1
Introduction

By the end of this Section you should be able to:

Understand Spreadsheet Design

Identify the Different Techniques to Use

Use Hyperlinks in Workbooks

To gain an understanding of the above features, work through the **Driving Lessons** in this **Section**.

For each **Driving Lesson**, read the **Park and Read** instructions, without touching the keyboard, then work through the numbered steps of the **Manoeuvres** on the computer. Complete the **S.A.E.** (Self-Assessment Exercise) at the end of the section to test your knowledge.

Driving Lesson 1 - Spreadsheet Design

Park and Read

Whilst any course on advanced spreadsheet applications needs to describe and explain the techniques necessary to produce successful worksheets, thought should always be given to the overall purpose of the finished spreadsheet and to the intended users.

Structure

Excel supports multi-sheet workbooks. A saved spreadsheet file is called a workbook. Each workbook can contain a vast number of worksheets. Each worksheet is a spreadsheet. Information can be passed from sheet to sheet, enabling large complicated models to be created using simpler smaller parts. For a company this is invaluable, different members of staff can provide data that feeds into a bigger picture worksheet, one where all the totals can be collected without the minute detail.

Purpose

Every worksheet produced has a purpose. Before starting to create a worksheet, take some time to consider the purpose behind it, how it will be used and the results that it needs to present, then plan the design accordingly.

Example 1. You are creating a spreadsheet to input and display departmental budgets and consolidate them into an overall company budget. Will each department complete its own piece of the worksheet, or will it be more efficient to have separate worksheets for each department and join them together later as a separate process? Will the results need to be incorporated into a larger financial report, in which case the formatting and structure will need to be compatible?

Example 2. You are creating a spreadsheet to record membership details for a club or gym. You need to know what the list will be used for. Does it need to record payment of fees? Will it be used to analyse membership over various activities or groups? If so, then relevant details need to be included. Will it be used to send out letters to members? If so, it will need to include names and addresses.

Example 3. You are creating a spreadsheet to present statistical viewing figures for a television channel. Does it need to show a series of charts without the original data, or just the data so that users can create their own charts? What analysis will be required? If it needs to be analysed by region for example, then regional information must be included with the original data.

Driving Lesson 1 - Continued

Audience

The intended users of your spreadsheet have a major impact on the way it is designed in two areas.

Firstly in the way it is presented. A company financial report for the Financial Director may need to have summary information analysed by various factors, using pivot tables and charts for example. The same data for an accountant or auditor may need to see the detailed breakdown of all totals into the individual items that make them up.

Secondly, many practical spreadsheets are dynamic, i.e. they will require frequent updating, and so users will be using your spreadsheet for data input and manipulation. Are your users going to merely read the data you give them, or are they expecting to analyse it themselves using filters and sorts for example. Make sure your design takes into account the competence of the people who will be doing this.

Other Considerations

There are often practical considerations to spreadsheet design. A working spreadsheet can in principle be as large as you like, but scrolling horizontally <u>and</u> vertically in a spreadsheet can become confusing. Try to arrange the layout so that scrolling is only necessary in one direction, or it may be better to split the solution into several linked worksheets where possible.

The final form of your spreadsheet may also affect its style. You may be asked to produce a spreadsheet that will be used on a web page or presentation slide. This will require that the final result is compact enough for this purpose.

Driving Lesson 2 - Techniques to Use

🄿 Park and Read

Spreadsheet software such as *Microsoft Excel* enables you to produce professional looking, functional worksheets for many different purposes. No matter what type of job you do, it's likely that at some stage you will need a list or table of data that requires some kind of manipulation or numerical processing, e.g. sorting, filtering or totalling and a spreadsheet would be the best solution for such a task.

In particular, *Excel* has many features that allow you to create complex spreadsheets, i.e. multi page sheets containing a variety of formatting styles and techniques and possibly containing various analysis and graphical presentation. Some of the relevant skills and techniques are:

- **Advanced editing and formatting**. Including custom and conditional formatting, hiding selected data and using subtotalling.

- **Templates**. Allowing many worksheets to be based on the same consistent style.

- **Security**. Restricting access to spreadsheets or protecting the content of certain cells within spreadsheets.

- **Linking**. Links to data within worksheets, between worksheets and between different workbooks.

- **Lists**. The specific features which can be used when the spreadsheet is in a list format.

- **Sorting**. Including custom sorts.

- **Querying/Filtering**. Including advanced options.

- **Charts and Graphs**. Including formatting and modifying of various chart types.

- **Functions**. Using a wide range of functions, including numerical, text, logical and lookup. Also includes complex formulas with nested functions.

- **Analysis techniques**. Including pivot tables, scenarios, and data tables.

- **Auditing**. Including error tracing, formula display and working with comments.

- **Macros**. Instructions to perform repetitive tasks with a single command.

- **Links**. To allow users of the documentation to access relevant data from other sources.

Driving Lesson 3 - Hyperlinks

Park and Read

When a spreadsheet is being viewed on screen, there are ways of making it easier for users to move to different locations within it, or to access connected information held in other locations. This is done using **hyperlinks**.

A hyperlink can be applied to a cell in a spreadsheet so that clicking the cell will display another location in the sheet which has been defined with a name. The hyperlink may also display a different worksheet, or open a different workbook. Alternatively the hyperlink could be used for reference purposes, opening a file from a different application or a web page.

Manoeuvres

1. Open the supplied data file **Hotel** (see page 4 - **Downloading the Data Files** for the location). This is a multi sheet workbook that has had names applied to some cell ranges. Make sure the **Accounts** sheet is displayed. Some hyperlinks will be added to this sheet.

2. Click on cell **G2**, **Profit**, select the **Insert** tab and click the **Hyperlink** button in the **Links** group.

3. Make sure **Place in This Document** is selected from the left of the dialog box, and if necessary click the ⊞ at the left of **Defined Names** to reveal the list of available names.

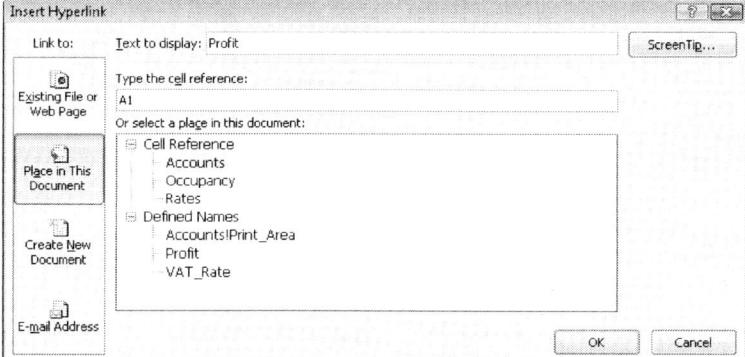

4. Select the name **Profit**. This has been defined as applying to the **Net Profit** figures, **B34:N34** on this sheet. Click **OK**.

Driving Lesson 3 - Continued

5.   Click on cell **H2**, **Rates**, and click the **Hyperlink** button.

6.   Make sure **Place in This Document** is still selected.

7.   The names under **Cell Reference** represent worksheet names in this workbook. Select the worksheet name **Rates** from this list and click **OK**.

8.   Click on cell **I2**, **Notes**, and click the **Hyperlink** button.

9.   Select **Existing File or Web Page** and **Current Folder**.

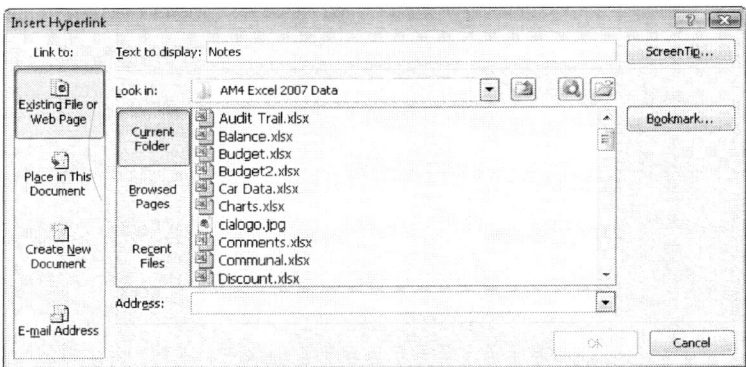

10. If necessary use the **Look in** box to locate the supplied data folder then select **Notes.docx** and click **OK**.

11. Click cell **J2**, **Consultants**, and click the **Hyperlink** button. Make sure **Existing File or Web Page** is selected.

12. Type **www.ciatraining.co.uk** in the **Address** box and click **OK**.

13. On the spreadsheet point and click on the hyperlinked text, **Profit**, in cell **G2**. The **Profit** range is displayed and highlighted.

14. Click the hyperlinked text, **Rates**, in cell **H2**. The **Rates** sheet is opened.

15. Return to the **Accounts** sheet and click **Notes** in cell **I2**. The notes document is opened in your word processing application.

16. Close the word processing application and click **Consultants** in cell **J2**. If you have a live Internet connection the CiA Training web site will be opened in your browser.

17. Close your browser.

18. Close the **Hotel** workbook <u>without</u> saving.

Driving Lesson 4 - S.A.E.

This is not an ECDL test. Testing may only be carried out through certified ECDL test centres. This is a Self-Assessment Exercise. Try to complete it without any reference to the Driving Lessons in this section.

1. When designing a spreadsheet, what are the advantages of splitting a large task into several smaller tasks using different worksheets/workbooks?

2. When designing a large spreadsheet why should it either fit horizontally or vertically on the screen, if possible?

3. When creating a spreadsheet for others why is protection of the data so important?

4. After creating a spreadsheet for others to use, what other tasks may you be required to do?

5. If you were a designer and seller of kitchens or bathrooms, what techniques might you use when creating supporting spreadsheets?

6. What is a template?

7. What is a macro?

8. If you were charged with assembling the sales figures for a company, how would you present them?

9. What is the difference between a link and a hyperlink?

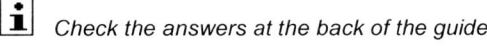 *Check the answers at the back of the guide.*

If you experienced any difficulty completing this S.A.E. refer back to the Driving Lessons in this section. Then redo the S.A.E.

Once you are confident with the features, complete the Record of Achievement Matrix referring to the section at the end of the guide. Only when competent move on to the next Section.

Section 2
Formatting

By the end of this Section you should be able to:

Freeze Titles

Use Conditional Formatting

Use AutoFormat

Use Paste Special

To gain an understanding of the above features, work through the **Driving Lessons** in this **Section**.

For each **Driving Lesson**, read the **Park and Read** instructions, without touching the keyboard, then work through the numbered steps of the **Manoeuvres** on the computer. Complete the **S.A.E.** (Self-Assessment Exercise) at the end of the section to test your knowledge.

Driving Lesson 5 - Freeze Titles

 Park and Read

The **Freeze Panes** command is used to keep particular rows and columns of information on the screen at all times. This is generally used so that the labels (titles) at the left of the rows and/or at the top of the columns are always seen, even while scrolling through the data in a worksheet.

 Manoeuvres

1.　Open the workbook **Retail**.

2.　Scroll to the right and note that the label column **A** disappears from view as the cursor scrolls off the screen.

3.　To keep column **A** on the screen at all times, the column must be frozen. Scroll column **A** back into view.

4.　Click on cell **B2** and from the **View** tab, **Window** group, click **Freeze Panes** and select **Freeze Panes**. This freezes **Row 1** and **Column A**.

i *Rows above the cursor and columns to the left of the cursor are frozen. The other options are Freeze Top Row or Freeze First Column.*

5.　Scroll to the right, the titles in column **A** remain on the screen, a very useful feature for large worksheets.

6.　Scroll down. The titles in **Row 1** remain frozen on the screen.

7.　Remove the frozen panes by selecting **Freeze Panes** then **Unfreeze Panes** from the **Window** group.

8.　Make the active cell **C1** and **Freeze** the panes again.

9.　Scroll to the right to see the new frozen titles. Scroll down: no rows are frozen.

10.　Select **Freeze Panes** then **Unfreeze Panes** from the **Window** group.

11.　Close the workbook <u>without</u> saving.

12.　Open the workbook **Spires**.

13.　Click on cell **A4** and freeze the panes. This freezes the top 3 rows only. Scroll down to see the effect.

14.　Scroll across, no columns are frozen.

15.　Unfreeze the panes.

16.　Close the workbook <u>without</u> saving.

Driving Lesson 6 - Conditional Formatting

Park and Read

As well as applying formatting to certain cells, it is possible to apply different formatting to cells depending on the values within those cells. Selected cells can be compared to a value, or the results of a formula, to decide which format should be used. This is called **Conditional Formatting**.

Multiple conditions can be used to determine the formatt ng for the same cell, so for example, a cell could be coloured red if it is below a certain value and blue if it is greater than another value.

Manoeuvres

1. Open the workbook **Retail**.

2. Highlight the **Turnover** figures, the range **B4:M4**.

3. With the **Home** tab displayed, from the **Styles** group, select **Conditional Formatting**. Select **New Rule**. The **New Formatting Rule** dialog box is displayed. Select **Format only cells that contain**.

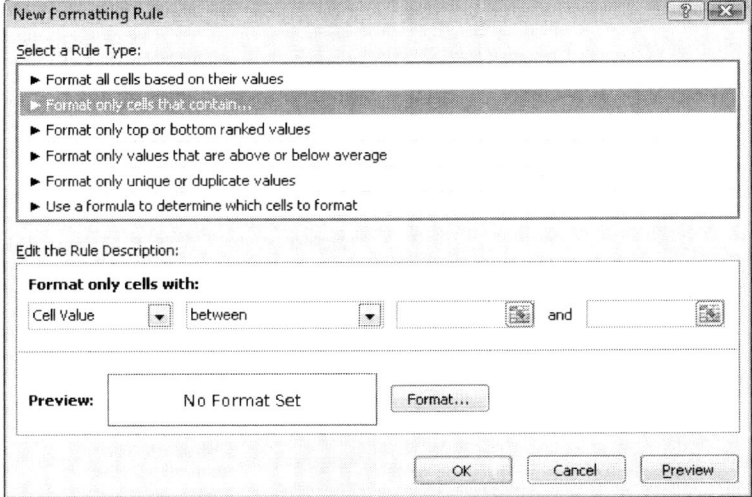

4. In the drop down criteria box (**between**) select **less than or equal to**. Enter the value **19000** in the next box.

Driving Lesson 6 - Continued

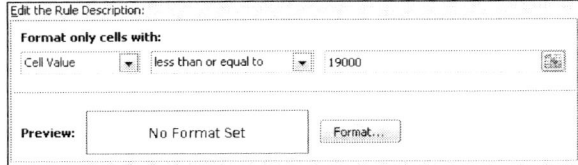

 If entering a formula in the value box remember to start with =

5. Click the **Format** button and select the **Font** colour **Red**. Click **OK**. Click **OK** again to apply the rule.

6. To add another condition to the same range, click the **Conditional Formatting** icon and select **New Rule**. Select **Format only cells that contain**, again. Select **greater than** and enter **25000** in the next box. Format the text to be **bold** and **blue**. Click **OK** and **OK** again to apply the formatting.

7. Highlight the range **B14:M14**, apply the conditional formatting, values **less than** the average of the range **=Average($B$14:$M$14)**. Format the range with a **pale yellow** cell shading using the **Fill** tab and **More Colors** option. Click **OK, OK** and **OK** again.

8. To remove **Conditional Formatting**, select the range **B4:M4**, click **Conditional Formatting** menu and select **Manage Rules**.

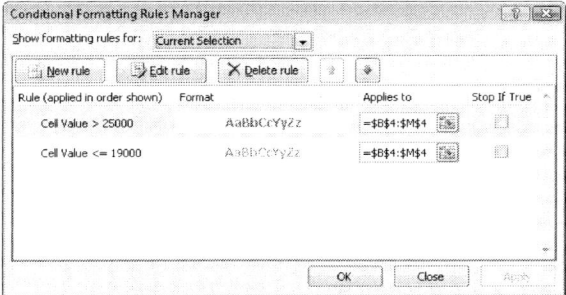

 The current selection has two rules applied to it. To view all the rules, select ***This Worksheet*** *from the* ***Show formatting rules for*** *box.*

9. Select the **Cell Value > 25000** rule and click the **Delete Rule** button, [✕ Delete rule]. Click **OK**. All values of over **25000** should now not be **blue** or **bold**.

10. Experiment with adding and removing conditional formats to experience the power of the feature to highlight results in a way that has not been possible before.

11. Close the workbook <u>without</u> saving.

Driving Lesson 7 - Format As Table

Park and Read

There is a set of pre-defined worksheet formats to enhance the appearance of a worksheet, via the **Home** tab **Styles** group, **Format As Table** command.

Manoeuvres

1. Open the workbook **Budget**.

2. Highlight the range **A1:N14** and on the **Home** tab, in the **Styles** group, click **Format as Table**.

3. There is a list of the available **Table Formats**, covering **Light**, **Medium** and **Dark** options. Scroll through the list of **Table Formats**. Select **Table Style Light 2**.

4. Click **OK**.

5. The sheet is now formatted in the **Light 2** style. A **Design** tab is displayed on the ribbon, showing various groups for different types of formatting.

6. To change the table format, select one from the **Table Styles** group on the **Design** tab. If this group is not displayed, click the **Quick Styles** button to display the available styles. The sheet displays each format as the mouse passes over it.

7. To remove the format, select the range **A1:N14**.

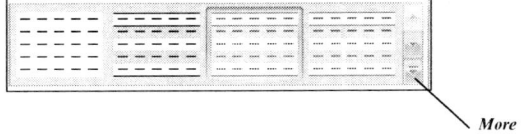

More

8. Using the **Design** tab, click the **More** button in the **Table Styles** group and then select **Clear**.

9. Close the workbook <u>without</u> saving.

Driving Lesson 8 - Paste Special

▣ Park and Read

When using **Copy** and **Paste** or **Cut** and **Paste**, the default is to paste the cell exactly as it was originally. **Paste Special** is used to paste cell information when a complete copy is not required. For example, **Paste Special** can:

> Paste only formulas, values or formats. Pasting values from cells that contain formulas is a way of fixing the data, as it will never then be recalculated.

> Combine ranges using an operation, e.g. adding, subtracting, etc.

> Transpose ranges (change a spreadsheet round by converting rows to columns and columns to rows).

> Paste links to the original data (covered in a later section).

⌁ Manoeuvres

1. Open the workbook **Finances**.

2. Highlight the range **A1:N1**. Change the range to italic and the font colour to blue.

3. To paste this formatting to another range, click the cell **A1** and in the **Home** tab, **Clipboard** group, click the **Copy** button.

4. Highlight the range **A2:A16** and select **Paste** drop down and select **Paste Special** to display the **Paste Special** dialog box.

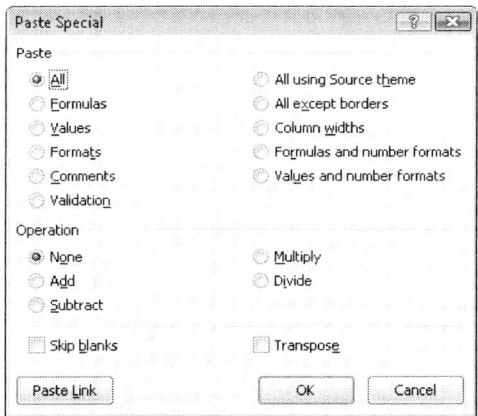

5. Under **Paste** select the **Formats** option and click **OK** to paste the formatting.

6. Open the workbook **Outgoings**.

Driving Lesson 8 - Continued

7.   Select the range **A1:L10** and click on the **Copy** button.

8.   Click on the icon representing the **Finances** workbook on the **Taskbar** to make it active.

9.   Click on cell **B5**. Click the **Paste** button to paste the contents normally.

 To avoid confusion, the data can be pasted to an empty area of the sheet and then moved.

10.   Data can be pasted using a mathematical operation. Open the file **Income** and highlight the range **A1:L2**, the income figures.

11.   Click the **Copy** button.

12.   Switch back to **Finances** using the **Taskbar**.

13.   The income figures are to go into the range **B2:M3** but this range already contains data, which would be overwritten if a normal paste was used. To keep the original data, select cell **B2** then click the **Paste** drop down and select **Paste Special**.

14.   Under **Operation** click **Add** to add the two sets of figures together, then click **OK**. The data is now combined.

 *The **Add** operation was used in this example. **Subtract**, **Multiply** and **Divide** work in the same way.*

15.   It may be required to convert formulas to values because the numbers are final, e.g. a VAT return or expenditure after the month end, etc. Using the **Finances** workbook, January has ended and the figures in column B are required to be converted to values. Check the cells **B4**, **B15** and **B16** to see that they contain formulas.

16.   Select the range **B2:B16**.

17.   Click **Copy**.

18.   Click the **Paste** drop down and select **Paste Special**.

19.   Under **Paste**, select the **Values** option and click **OK**. Click away from the selection.

20.   Check that the cells **B4**, **B15** and **B16** contain values.

 Remember that this process removes formulas and therefore the worksheet cannot be used again. If repeated use is required, create and use a template.

21.   Save the workbook as **Finances2** and close it.

22.   Close the workbooks **Income** and **Outgoings** without saving.

Driving Lesson 9 - S.A.E.

This is not an ECDL test. Testing may only be carried out through certified ECDL test centres. This is a Self-Assessment Exercise. Try to complete it without any reference to the Driving Lessons in this section.

1. Open the workbook **House**.

2. Format the range **B2:N16** as currency with two decimal places.

3. Freeze the column and row titles.

4. Scroll off the screen to check that the titles are frozen.

5. Format the whole worksheet in **Table Style Medium 3**.

6. The screen is cluttered, change the row height of rows **2** to **16** to **15.00** units.

7. The screen is now cluttered with zeros, reformat the range **B2:N16** as **Currency** with no decimal places, to remove some of them.

8. Apply conditional formatting to the range **B16:N16** the accumulated savings row, to display amounts greater than **1000** to be bold and displayed in blue text and saving levels under **0** in bold and displayed in red text.

9. An unexpected windfall comes in the form of a **£500** pay bonus in **February**. Make the necessary change. Note the effects of the conditional formatting on row **16**.

10. Highlight the whole worksheet, range **A1:N16** and using paste special make a copy on **Sheet2** but paste only the values.

11. Check the cells in rows **4**, **15** and **16** that contained formulas but are now just numbers. Change cell **B2** to **0**. It has no impact on any other cells.

12. Save the workbook as **House2**.

13. Close the workbook.

If you experienced any difficulty completing this S.A.E. refer back to the Driving Lessons in this section. Then redo the S.A.E.

Once you are confident with the features, complete the Record of Achievement Matrix referring to the section at the end of the guide. Only when competent move on to the next Section.

Section 3
Protection

By the end of this Section you should be able to:

Protect Cells

Hide and Unhide Columns and Rows

Create Read-Only Workbooks

Hide and Unhide Windows

Protect Workbooks

To gain an understanding of the above features, work through the **Driving Lessons** in this **Section**.

For each **Driving Lesson**, read the **Park and Read** instructions, without touching the keyboard, then work through the numbered steps of the **Manoeuvres** on the computer. Complete the **S.A.E.** (Self-Assessment Exercise) at the end of the section to test your knowledge.

Driving Lesson 10 - Protection

🅿 Park and Read

Varying levels of protection can be applied to workbooks, individual worksheets and cells within worksheets. Opening sensitive files or data can be controlled by using passwords, either by preventing access completely or allowing files to be examined but not amended (Read Only access).

Specific areas within spreadsheets can be protected from accidental or deliberate alteration, by applying cell locking.

The following protection is available:

Passwords   prevent the workbooks from being opened by unauthorised users.

Cell Locking   prevents important cell data (usually formulas) from being amended or deleted. Cell locking is only activated when worksheet protection is switched on.

Workbooks   can have passwords added to them. They can be made **Read Only** to prevent changes.

Worksheets   can have cells locked to prevent changes and optionally, a password added to protect locked data and worksheet structure. A protected worksheet can only have data entered into unlocked cells and formatting cannot be carried out. When worksheet protection is disabled (the default) all cells are accessible whether locked or not.

Driving Lesson 11 - Worksheet & Cell Protection

 Park and Read

Worksheets can be protected with passwords so that no changes can be made to the locked cells within them.

By default all cells on a worksheet are locked, but this has no effect until worksheet protection is activated.

To allow changes to be made to some cells but not others when the worksheet is protected, it is necessary to unlock the editable cells, prior to adding the protection. This is often used when providing a spreadsheet for other users for data entry. All titles and formulas are locked to prevent changes, and only the cells where data is to be entered are unlocked and therefore accessible.

Manoeuvres

1.   Open the workbook **Invoices**.

2.   To protect the worksheet from changes, from the **Home** tab, **Cells** group, select **Format** then click **Protect Sheet**.

3.   Entering a password is optional (be careful when using passwords as access to worksheets is prohibited without the password). Type **pass**. The password appears as ******** it is not displayed on the screen. Click **OK**.

 Passwords are case sensitive.

Driving Lesson 11 - Continued

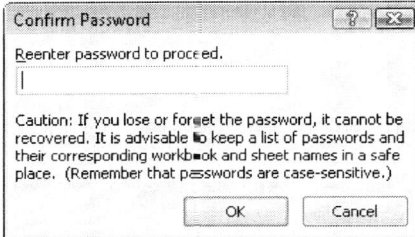

4.   Confirm the password by typing **pass** again. Click **OK**.

5.   Click on any cell and try to enter some data. No changes can be made to any cell on the worksheet. *Excel* displays the following message.

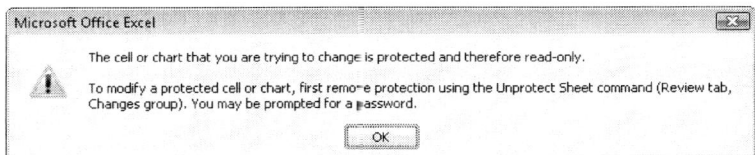

6.   Click **OK**.

7.   To remove the protection, display the **Format** drop down list and select **Unprotect Sheet**. Enter the password **pass** and click **OK** to remove the worksheet protection.

8.   To allow changes to cells on a protected sheet, the required cells must first be **unlocked**. Select the range **E6:E14**. These are the cells that may be changed after protection has been added.

9.   Display the **Format** drop down list and click **Lock Cell**. The protection of the range is now unlocked.

10. Having unlocked the required cells to take effect, the worksheet has to be protected. Re-protect the sheet.

Remember that a password is optional and can be omitted, but the protection can then be removed by using the Unprotect Sheet command.

11. Enter the password **pass** and click **OK**.

12. Confirm the password by typing **pass** again. Click **OK**.

13. Move to **E7** and change the contents to **£1500.00**.

14. Move to **F7** and try to change the **VAT** to **£250**. This cell is locked. Only the **Amount** column may be changed, i.e. the range **E6:E14**, that was unlocked previously. Click **OK**.

15. Change cell **E10** to **750**. This is allowed as the cell is unlocked.

16. Close the workbook **Invoices** <u>without</u> saving the changes.

Driving Lesson 12 - Hiding Rows & Columns

▣ Park and Read

Rows and/or **Columns** of sensitive data can be hidden from view. The data in any hidden rows and columns is still included in calculations, so that the results of the sheet are unaffected.

〽 Manoeuvres

1.   Open the workbook **Budget**.

2.   Highlight the rows **5** and **6**. From the **Home** tab, **Cells** group, display the **Format** drop down list select **Hide & Unhide** then **Hide Rows**. Rows 5 and 6 have now been hidden.

	A	B	C	D	E	F
1	Budget	Jan	Feb	Mar	Apr	May
2	Sales	6000	6400	7200	6200	5300
3	Price	6	6	6	6	6
4	Turnover	36000	38400	43200	37200	31800
7	Wages	6400	6400	6400	6400	6400
8	Materials	20800	22400	25600	21600	18000
9	Overheads	5000	5000	5000	5000	5000

Rows 5 and 6 are hidden. Note that row 7 still calculates Wages.

3.   To re-display rows **5** and **6**, highlight a range in row **4** to row **7**, e.g. **A4:A7** and from the **Format** drop down list select **Hide & Unhide** then **Unhide Rows**.

4.   A column can be hidden in a similar way, but another method is to use the shortcut menu. Right click on the column heading **F** and select **Hide** from the shortcut menu.

5.   To re-display column **F**, select columns **E** to **G**, right click and select **Unhide**.

6.   Columns and rows may also be hidden by dragging their borders until the column width or the row height is zero. To hide column **M** using this method, place the mouse pointer on the column divider between **M** and **N**. Drag the adjust cursor to the left, carefully, till the column width is **0.00**.

ⓘ *Dragging further left hides multiple columns. If this happens, use **Undo** to restore the columns and try again.*

7.   The mouse can also be used to unhide columns or rows. There are two adjust cursors. The normal column adjust cursor is on the left or for a row is above. To the right of a hidden column or below a hidden row the adjust cursor changes to ⁺‖⁺ or ⬥. Dragging this cursor redisplays the hidden data. Unhide column **M** making it **10.00 (75 pixels)** wide.

8.   Close the workbook <u>without</u> saving.

Driving Lesson 13 - Workbook Protection

Park and Read

Workbooks may contain sensitive or private data which means that the whole workbook has to be kept secure. **Passwords** can be assigned to workbooks so that only those people who know the password can open them.

Manoeuvres

1.   Open the workbook **Retail**.

2.   Click the **Office** button then select **Save As**. From the **Save As** dialog box click the **Tools** button and select **General Options**.

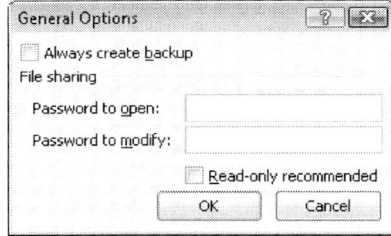

3.   In the **Password to open** box, type **PASS** (passwords are case-sensitive. **PASS** is not the same as **pass** or **Pass**), then click on **OK**. Note that the letters do not appear as you type, only asterisks.

 Choose a password that is easily remembered, but not so obvious that it can be easily guessed. If passwords are forgotten, the workbook cannot be opened, so the data within all the sheets is lost!

4.   To confirm the password, it must be re-entered. Enter it, then click **OK**.

5.   In the **Save As** dialog box, enter **Secure** in the **File name** box, then click **Save**.

6.   Close the workbook **Secure** and open it again. A prompt for the password will be displayed. Try typing in an **Incorrect** password and clicking **OK**.

7.   Repeat step 6, this time entering the correct password, **PASS**. Click **OK**.

8.   To remove the password protection, click the **Office** button, then **Save As**. Click the **Tools** button and then select **General Options**. Delete the asterisks in the **Password to open** box, click **OK** and save the file under the same name, replacing the existing workbook.

9.   Close the workbook.

Driving Lesson 14 - Hiding Worksheets & Workbooks

Park and Read

A workbook or a worksheet can be hidden, when the contents are needed but are not to be seen. Hidden worksheets and the workbook still remain open.

Manoeuvres

1. Open the workbooks **Spires** and **Budget**.

2. With **Budget** in the active workbook select the **View** tab and in the **Window** group click **Hide** (button to the right of **Arrange All**). This hides the whole workbook.

3. Check the **Taskbar** for **Budget** and the **Switch Windows** menu for open workbooks. **Budget** is not displayed in either.

4. Select **Unhide** from the **Window** group (to the right of **Freeze Panes**).

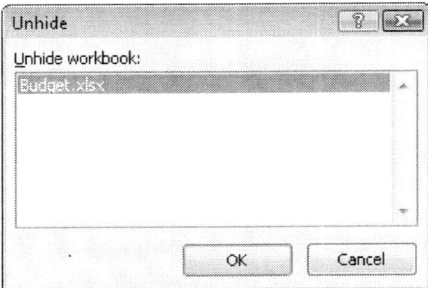

5. **Budget** is the only hidden window. Click **OK** to restore it.

6. Make **Spires** active. Click on the **Rates** sheet. This sheet contains the **Tax** and **Vat** rates.

7. Using the **Home** tab, **Cells** group, select **Format** then **Hide & Unhide** then **Hide Sheet**. The **Rates** sheet is no longer visible, although the contents are used in the **Accounts** sheet.

8. The sheet is hidden until it is restored. Saving the workbook leaves the sheet hidden. Using the **Home** tab, **Cells** group, select **Format** then **Hide & Unhide** and finally **Unhide Sheet**.

9. With the **Rates** sheet selected, click **OK** to restore it.

10. Close all the open workbooks <u>without</u> saving.

Driving Lesson 15 - S.A.E.

This is not an ECDL test. Testing may only be carried out through certified ECDL test centres. This is a Self-Assessment Exercise. Try to complete it without any reference to the Driving Lessons in this section.

1.　Open the workbook **Easy**. All cells in the worksheet have been **unlocked**.

2.　This worksheet stretches from **A1** to **N14**, but has some data hidden. Unhide the data so that the full worksheet is visible.

3.　Make the following ranges **locked**:

> **B4:M4**
> **B10:M10**
> **B14:M14**
> **N1:N14**

4.　Add the sheet protection without a password.

5.　Enter the **Password to open** as **Pass** and save the workbook as **Protect**.

6.　Close the workbook.

7.　Open the workbook **Protect**.

8.　Remove the workbook password and add the password **007** as a **Password to modify**. Click **Yes** to Replace the existing file.

9.　Close the workbook.

10.　Open the workbook **Protect**, enter the password **007** to be able to modify.

11.　Remove the password and save the workbook using the same file name without any password protection. At the prompt to replace the existing file select **Yes**.

12.　Close the workbook, saving with the same file name.

If you experienced any difficulty completing this S.A.E. refer back to the Driving Lessons in this section. Then redo the S.A.E.

Once you are confident with the features, complete the Record of Achievement Matrix referring to the section at the end of the guide. Only when competent move on to the next Section.

Section 4

Cell Comments

By the end of this Section you should be able to:

Use Cell Comments

Display Comments

Create, Edit and Delete Comments

To gain an understanding of the above features, work through the **Driving Lessons** in this **Section**.

For each **Driving Lesson**, read the **Park and Read** instructions, without touching the keyboard, then work through the numbered steps of the **Manoeuvres** on the computer. Complete the **S.A.E.** (Self-Assessment Exercise) at the end of the section to test your knowledge.

Driving Lesson 16 - Cell Comments

 Park and Read

A **Comment** is a piece of text that is attached to a cell. Depending on which options are set, comments are not usually displayed on the worksheet, but a **comment indicator** (a small red triangle) shows where the comments are. They can be easily viewed by moving the mouse pointer over the relevant cell.

 Manoeuvres

1.　Open the workbook **Comments**.

2.　Some of the cells on the sheet have red triangles in the corners. These cells have comments attached. Place the mouse pointer on cell **D7**, which has a comment indicator (a small red triangle).

3.　Leave the mouse pointer over the cell for a while and a box will appear containing the comment for that cell.

Division	Sales	Profit	Employees
North	£112,000	Very impressive sales. Pay a bonus.	
South	£97,456		
East	£102,765		
West	£66,833		

i　*If the comment indicator cannot be seen, click the **Office** button then the **Excel Options** button and in the **Advanced** section under **Display** select the required option. The **No comments or indicators** option hides both the comments and indicators, **Comments and indicators** option displays both, select the **Indicators only, and comments on hover** option and click **OK**.*

4.　Place the mouse over the other cells containing comments in turn and view them.

5.　Leave the workbook **Comments** open.

Driving Lesson 17 - Display Comments

▣ Park and Read

Comments can be set to display permanently. The **Review** tab is used to manipulate the comments.

ℝ Manoeuvres

1. The workbook **Comments** should still be open. If not, open it.

2. Display the **Review** tab and in the **Comments** group click the **Show All Comments** button.

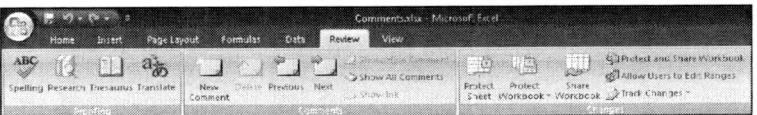

3. The **Show All Comments** button displays or hides all the comments. Click the **Show All Comments** button again, all the comments are hidden.

4. To show the **Comments** in turn, the **Next**, or **Previous** buttons are used. Click in cell **A1**. Click the **Next** button. This displays the **Comment** in **D7** in **Edit** mode.

5. Use the **Next** and **Previous** buttons to scroll from comment to comment. An information message is displayed when the end or beginning of the workbook is reached. Click **OK** if this message is displayed.

6. Click on cell **D7** and click the **Show/Hide Comment** button, ⬛ Show/Hide Comment. This displays an individual comment permanently until hidden. (The same button also hides a displayed comment).

7. Right click on cell **D7** and select **Hide Comment**.

ℹ️ *Comments can be shown or hidden using the **Review** tab (for multiple comments) or the **Shortcut Menu** from a cell (for a single comment).*

8. Leave the workbook **Comments** open.

Driving Lesson 18 - Create, Edit and Delete Comments

Park and Read

Comments can be inserted anywhere in a spreadsheet and any text can be added. Text in comments can be edited and comments can be deleted.

Manoeuvres

1. The workbook **Comments** should still be open. İf not, open it.

2. To create a comment attached to cell **E10**, right click on **E10** and select **Insert Comment** from the shortcut menu.

 *Alternatively click on the cell and then click the **New Comment** button, on the **Review** tab.*

3. In the **Comment** box, the user name is added automatically to the top line of the comment, delete it and type **We must improve this figure**.

4. Adjust the size of the **Comment Box** (using the handles). Move the box away from the numbers, by placing the cursor on any edge and clicking and dragging (the cursor changes to a four headed arrow when over the box).

5. Click away from the comment to complete it. The comment indicator is now displayed in the cell **E10**.

6. Move the mouse over cell **E10** to display the **Comment**. The temporary display is next to the cell.

7. Move the mouse on to cell **D7** and display that **Comment**. Right click on cell **D7** and select **Edit Comment**.

 *Alternatively select **Edit Comment** from the **Comments** group.*

8. Use the <**Backspace**> key to delete the second sentence and edit the comment to **We cannot afford a bonus**. Reduce the size of the comment box and move it away from the numbers.

9. To remove the note attached to cell **F7**, right click on cell **F7** and select **Delete Comment**. The comment is deleted and the comment indicator is removed.

10. Close the workbook **Comments** <u>without</u> saving.

Driving Lesson 19 - S.A.E.

This is not an ECDL test. Testing may only be carried out through certified ECDL test centres. This is a Self-Assessment Exercise. Try to complete it without any reference to the Driving Lessons in this section.

1. Open the workbook **Budget**.

2. Add the comment **Why the sudden drop in sales?** to cell **J2**.

3. Add the comment **Consider increasing the price?** to cell **B3**.

4. Add the comment **Too many employees?** to cell **B5**.

5. Add the comment **This loss needs to be turned into a profit!** to cell **J14**.

6. Using the **Page Layout** tab change the page to **Landscape**. Click the **Page Setup** dialog box launcher and select **Fit to** one page. Under the **Sheet** tab, select **At end of sheet** from the **Comments** area. **Print** a copy of the worksheet and the comments.

7. **Show** all the comments on the worksheet.

8. **Hide** the comment attached to cell **J2**.

9. Edit the comment in cell **J14** to read **This loss at the end of year needs to be turned into a profit.**

10. **Delete** the comment attached to cell **B3**.

11. **Hide** all displayed comments.

12. Close the workbook <u>without</u> saving.

If you experienced any difficulty completing this S.A.E. refer back to the Driving Lessons in this section. Then redo the S.A.E.

Once you are confident with the features, complete the Record of Achievement Matrix referring to the section at the end of the guide. Only when competent move on to the next Section.

Section 5
Names

By the end of this Section you should be able to:

Use Names

Create Names from Ranges

Paste and Apply Names

Use Names in Formulas

Use Names with Go To

To gain an understanding of the above features, work through the **Driving Lessons** in this **Section**.

For each **Driving Lesson**, read the **Park and Read** instructions, without touching the keyboard, then work through the numbered steps of the **Manoeuvres** on the computer. Complete the **S.A.E.** (Self-Assessment Exercise) at the end of the section to test your knowledge.

Driving Lesson 20 - Names

Park and Read

Names can be used to represent the contents of a cell or a range of cells to make referencing them easier.

For example, a formula might be **=D34-D67**, and the cell references would have to be traced back to see what they represent. If **D34** represents income and **D67** represents expenditure, **Names** could be used so that the same formula can be entered as:

= Income - Expenditure

making it easier for anyone viewing the formula to understand what it is.

Any cell in a worksheet can be given a name by using the **Define Name** command. For this name to be used as a reference in formulas, the command **Apply Names** must be used.

Manoeuvres

1. Open the workbook **Vat**.

2. In **C6** enter the formula to calculate the **VAT**. Remember, this will have to use **Absolute Addressing**. The formula is **=C5*$B$15**.

3. Copy this formula across the row into **D6** and **E6**. Complete the **Total Price** row, adding the **Price** to the **VAT**.

4. Click on cell **B15**, the **VAT Rate**. Enter the new rate of **17.5%** (include the **%** sign).

5. The use of **Names** would make the formulas in this worksheet easier to understand. Click on cell **B15** and from the **Formulas** tab, select **Define Name** from the **Defined Names** group.

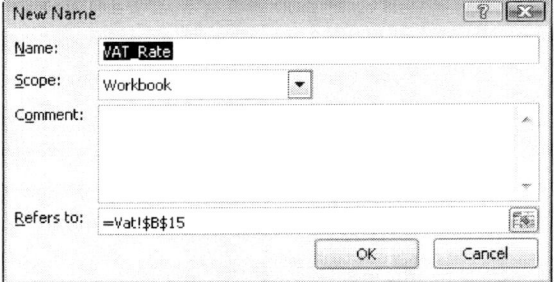

Driving Lesson 20 - Continued

6. The **New Name** dialog box shows any **Names** already defined in the workbook (none in this case) and may suggest a name for the selected cell (**VAT_Rate**). It also displays where the name **Refers to** (Vat!$B$15). The suggested name may be overwritten, but as **VAT_Rate** is a suitable name, click **OK**.

 *New Name picks its suggestions from any nearby labels but replaces spaces with underscores as spaces are not allowed in **Names**. If there are no suitable suggestions the **Name** box will be blank.*

7. Note that the **Cell Reference Area** now contains the name of the cell, **VAT_Rate** (above the column **A** heading). Move to cell **C6**. The cell contents still reference **$B$15**. The cell has been named but the name is not used anywhere yet.

8. Select **Apply Names** from the **Define Name** drop down list.

9. A list of available names is displayed, but in this case, just **VAT_Rate**. Click on **OK** to apply this name to the worksheet.

10. Note that the reference for **C6** now shows **C5*VAT_Rate**. The other **VAT** cells are similar.

11. Save the workbook as **Vat2**.

12. Leave the workbook open for the next Driving Lesson.

Driving Lesson 21 - Using Names in Formulas

Park and Read

As well as manually defining **Names** for individual cells, they can be automatically created for ranges of cells based on existing row and column headers, using the **Create from Selection** button.

Existing **Names** can be used in new formulas by typing the cell name or by using the **Use in Formula** drop down **Paste** command.

Manoeuvres

1. Open the workbook **Vat2** if it is not already open.

2. Select the range **B4:E7**.

3. Click the **Create from Selection** button.

4. Make sure **Top Row** and **Left Column** are selected. Click **OK** to create names based on the row and column headers for the selected range.

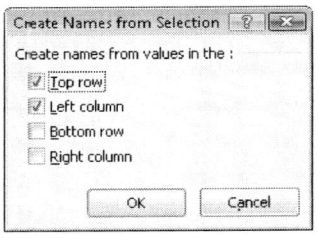

5. Select **Apply Names** from the **Define Name** drop down to display all the names just created. The new names should be highlighted. Click **OK** to apply these names to all formulas.

6. Select **C7** to see names used in the formula rather than cell references. Look at other cells containing formulas.

7. Insert a column between **March** and **Total**. In **F4** enter **April** and in **F5** type **5050**.

8. In **F6** type **=F5*** and then click **Use in Formula**.

9. Select **VAT_Rate** from the displayed list. The name is pasted into the formula. Press **<Enter>** to complete the formula.

10. Enter the appropriate formula in **F7** to add the **Total Price** for April. Note that as **Column F** was added after creating the names it is not included in the named ranges.

 To include names in the new column, the names have to be redefined. It is better to leave the creating and applying of names till after the spreadsheet structure has been completed.

11. Check the formulas in the **Total** column to make sure that they include the new figures.

12. Leave the workbook **Vat2** open for the next Driving Lesson.

Driving Lesson 22 - Using Go To with Names

Park and Read

The **Go To** command can not only be used to move quickly to a cell by typing its reference, but also to move to any named cell or range.

Manoeuvres

1. Open the workbook **Vat2** if it is not already open.

2. Display the **Home** tab and from the **Editing** group, select **Go To** from the **Find & Select** drop down.

 *Alternatively the key press <**Ctrl G**> or the function key <**F5**> can be used*

3. All the names on the sheet are listed. Click **VAT_Rate**, the name applied to a single cell, and then **OK**.

4. The cell containing the **VAT_Rate**, i.e. **B15**, is now the active cell.

5. Press <**F5**>, the **Go To** key. Select **January** from the list and click **OK**. The range of cells named **January** is highlighted.

6. Close the workbook <u>without</u> saving.

7. Open the workbook **Budget2**.

8. Press <**F5**>, the **Go To** key. There is a long list of all the named ranges in this sheet. Select **Materials** then **OK**. The range containing the **Materials** figures will be highlighted. Use the horizontal scroll bar to view the whole range if necessary.

9. Select **Go To** from the **Find & Select** drop down, choose **May** and click **OK**. The figures for **May** are now highlighted.

10. Close the workbook <u>without</u> saving.

Driving Lesson 23 - S.A.E.

This is not an ECDL test. Testing may only be carried out through certified ECDL test centres. This is a Self-Assessment Exercise. Try to complete it without any reference to the Driving Lessons in this section.

1.　Open the workbook **Retail**.

2.　Define names for the whole worksheet, i.e. **A1:N14.**

3.　Apply the names just created.

4.　Move to cell **P3** and type **=Sales Feb** to find the sales figure for **February**.

5.　What is the sales figure for **February**?

6.　Similarly, in cell **P5**, what is the amount of **Spending** in **April (Apr)**?

7.　**Go To** the **Sales** figures and format the named range **bold**.

8.　Close the workbook <u>without</u> saving.

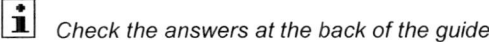 *Check the answers at the back of the guide.*

If you experienced any difficulty completing this S.A.E. refer back to the Driving Lessons in this section. Then redo the S.A.E.

Once you are confident with the features, complete the Record of Achievement Matrix referring to the section at the end of the guide. Only when competent move on to the next Section.

Section 6
Templates

By the end of this Section you should be able to:

Create and Understand Templates

Use Templates

Edit Templates

Delete Templates

To gain an understanding of the above features, work through the **Driving Lessons** in this **Section**.

For each **Driving Lesson**, read the **Park and Read** instructions, without touching the keyboard, then work through the numbered steps of the **Manoeuvres** on the computer. Complete the **S.A.E.** (Self-Assessment Exercise) at the end of the section to test your knowledge.

Driving Lesson 24 - Creating a Template

▣ Park and Read

A **Template** is a base worksheet that has been prepared ready for data to be entered. It can contain: text, graphics, formulas, protection, macros and formatting. Using a template ensures consistency of appearance and performance for the spreadsheets based on it.

Templates are created by specifying a **Save as type** of **Template** when saving. They are given a file extension of **.xltx** which distinguishes them from normal workbooks.

👆 Manoeuvres

1. Open the workbook **Budget**. This represents the budget data for a small company.

2. To change this workbook into a template, the base data must be removed, leaving the formulas. Delete the data in the ranges **B2:M3**, **B5:M6** and **B8:M9**.

3. To save this workbook as a **Template**, click the **Office** button and select **Save As** from the menu.

4. In the **Save as type**, choose **Excel Template**.

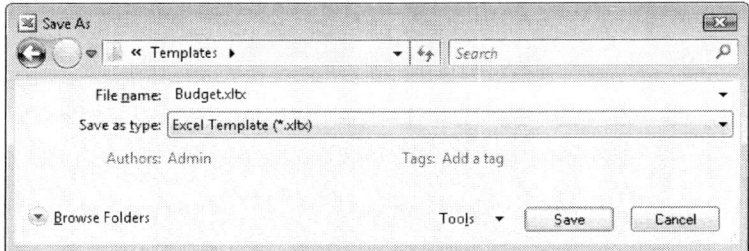

5. Notice how the location for the saved file changes automatically to the **Templates** folder. Click **Save**. The workbook is then saved as a template and stored with other templates.

6. Close the **Budget** workbook.

Driving Lesson 25 - Using a Template

Park and Read

A template can be opened repeatedly and used as the base for many other spreadsheets. These are saved as workbooks with new names to leave the original template unaffected.

Manoeuvres

1. To use a template, click the **Office** button and then **New**.

2. The **New Workbook** dialog box is displayed. Click **My templates**.

3. Click **Budget** and then **OK**.

4. The **template** is opened and the name changed to **Budget1**. Data can now be added. Add some data to column **B** to see if the formulas work.

5. The name **Budget1** is similar in use to the default workbook names **Book1**, etc. To save the template as a workbook, click the **Office** button and select either **Save** or **Save As** to display the **Save As** dialog box.

6. Save the workbook as **Budget2006** (take care to save to the required location not the **Templates** folder).

7. Open the **Budget** template again and then compare the open workbooks by making each one active in turn.

8. Close both the workbooks <u>without</u> saving.

Driving Lesson 26 - Editing a Template

 Park and Read

If required, templates can be resaved as templates with the same file name, allowing the original template to be overwritten to incorporate changes.

Manoeuvres

1. Start a **New** workbook based on the **Budget** template.

2. Change all the tax rates to **40**%.

3. Change the orientation of the page to landscape and ensure that the spreadsheet fits onto one page.

4. Format the numbers within rows **2 to 4, 6 to 11, 13 & 14** as currency with 2 decimal places.

5. To resave the template, click the **Office** button and then select **Save As**.

6. Change the **Save as type** to **Excel Template (*.xltx)** and enter the file name **Budget**.

7. Click **Save**.

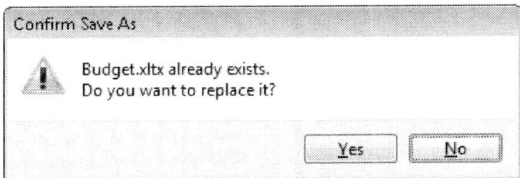

8. A dialog box appears informing that the **Budget** file already exists, click **Yes** to overwrite the original template.

9. Close the **Budget** template.

10. Open a copy of the template to check that the changes have been made.

11. Close all open workbooks.

Driving Lesson 27 - Deleting Templates

 Park and Read

Templates that are no longer needed, can be deleted. Caution must be taken when deleting a template to make sure that the correct one is selected.

Manoeuvres

1. **Templates** are available to all users of the computer. The templates are stored on the **C:** drive. The **template** created and used in the last three lessons is to be deleted. Click the **Office** button and then **New**.

2. Click **My templates**. The templates are displayed with icons (a yellow stripe along the top of a pad of pages). Right click on **Budget** and from the shortcut menu select **Delete**.

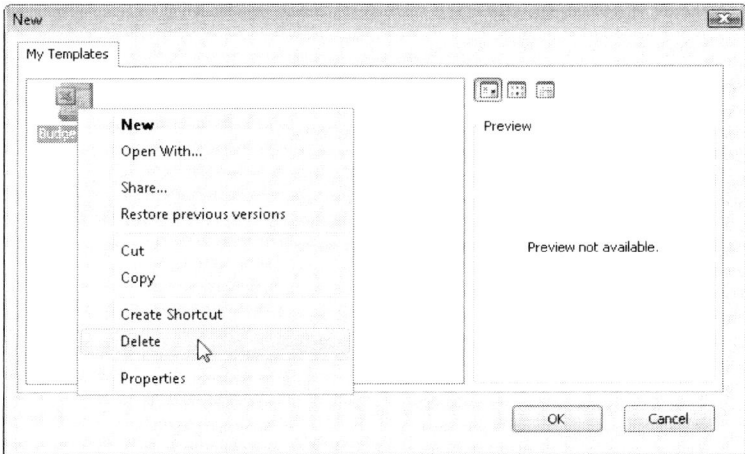

3. At the message prompt, click **Yes** to confirm the deletion.

4. Click **Cancel** to close the **New** dialog box.

5. Click **Cancel** to close the **New Workbook** dialog box.

Driving Lesson 28 - S.A.E.

This is not an ECDL test. Testing may only be carried out through certified ECDL test centres. This is a Self-Assessment Exercise. Try to complete it without any reference to the Driving Lessons in this section.

1. Open the workbook **Retail** and delete all the values on rows **2**, **3** and **5** to **9**, be careful not to delete the formulas in column **N**.

2. Save the workbook as a **Template**, using the same name and close it.

3. Open the **Retail** template.

4. To add data to the template, open the workbook **Retail Data**.

5. Copy and paste the data in range **A3:L4** from **Retail Data** to **B2** in **Retail** and the range **A6:L10** to **B5**.

6. Save the workbook as **Retail2**.

7. Close the workbook. Close **Retail Data**.

8. The **Retail** template is to be deleted. Display the **templates** on your computer.

9. Right click on the **Retail** template and select **Delete**.

10. Click **Yes** to confirm the deletion.

11. Check that the template **Retail** has been deleted.

12. Cancel any open dialog boxes.

If you experienced any difficulty completing this S.A.E. refer back to the Driving Lessons in this section. Then redo the S.A.E.

Once you are confident with the features, complete the Record of Achievement Matrix referring to the section at the end of the guide. Only when competent move on to the next Section.

Section 7
Formulas

By the end of this Section you should be able to:

Display and Check Formulas

Understand Formulas that Produce Errors

Create Custom Number Formats

To gain an understanding of the above features, work through the **Driving Lessons** in this **Section**.

For each **Driving Lesson**, read the **Park and Read** instructions, without touching the keyboard, then work through the numbered steps of the **Manoeuvres** on the computer. Complete the **S.A.E.** (Self-Assessment Exercise) at the end of the section to test your knowledge.

Driving Lesson 29 - Display Formulas

▣ Park and Read

It is sometimes useful to identify quickly which cells within a worksheet are formulas rather than entered values, and to display the actual formulas on the screen instead of the results. This is particularly relevant when checking whether all formulas are correct. Individual formulas can also be displayed in a way that aids checking.

⌐ Manoeuvres

1.   Open the workbook **Balance**.

2.   To determine which cells in the worksheet are formulas, display the **Home** tab and from the **Editing** group, select **Find & Replace** then **Go To Special**.

3.   Select **Formulas** and click **OK**. All formula cells are highlighted, showing for example that the numbers in the **Charities** row are not simply entered values but the results of calculations.

4.   To display all the formulas on a worksheet use the key press combination **<Ctrl `>**. Press the **Ctrl** and the key under the **Esc** key. All formulas will be shown in full, the columns being widened where necessary.

5.   Press **< Ctrl `>** again to revert to the normal view (results rather than formulas).

 *Alternatively all formulas may be displayed by selecting **Excel Options**, from the **Office** menu. In the **Advanced** section check **Show formulas in cells instead of their calculated results** under **Display options for this worksheet**. Click **OK**.*

6.   Ensure that the worksheet is in normal view and double click on cell **D16**. The formula is displayed in the cell itself with colour coding to show which cells or ranges are used in the formula. So the reference to **C16** is in blue and the cell **C16** is outlined in blue.

7.   The worksheet is in **In-cell edit** mode now so that the formula can be amended, by dragging the coloured outlines to different cells or by dragging the **Fill Handle** to extend the range. After checking, press **<Enter>** (to accept any changes) or **<Esc>** (to reject any changes) to finish the editing.

8.   Leave the workbook **Balance** open.

Driving Lesson 30 - Formulas that Produce Errors

▣ Park and Read

There can be problems when some formulas are calculated, usually because the referenced cells are not as expected. When a formula cannot be calculated the cell displays an error message. Functions **ISERROR** and **ERROR.TYPE** can be used to check for and identify errors.

The following error values (with their error type number) can be found:

#NULL!	1	The two areas specified do not intersect
#DIV/0!	2	Division by zero
#VALUE!	3	The wrong argument used
#REF!	4	Cell referenced is not valid
#NAME?	5	Does not recognise text in a formula
#NUM!	6	Error with number in formula
#N/A	7	The value used in the formula is not available
######		The result is too long to fit into the cell

⌐ Manoeuvres

1. The workbook **Balance** should still be open. If not, open it.

2. In cell **H20** enter the function **=ISERROR(H18)** to check whether the formula in **H18** is producing an error. It should read **FALSE**.

3. In cell **H4**, enter the number **0**. Cell **H18** is now a **#DIV/0!** error because it is trying to divide by **H4**. **H20** should read **TRUE**.

4. Cell **H18** is displayed with a green triangle. Click on cell **H18**, a **Smart Tag** is displayed, ⬦.

5. Click on the tag to display a list of options.

6. The error is shown as a **Divide by Zero Error**. Investigate the available options.

7. Using the function **IF** can replace errors with a specific value. In cell **H18** enter the formula **=IF(H4=0,0,H16/H4)**. If **H4** is zero the formula is not calculated (so no error and **H20 = FALSE** again) and the value of **0** is returned.

8. In cell **H4**, enter the character **X**. Cells **H16** and **H18** are now **#VALUE!** errors because both expect cell **H4** to be a numeric value.

9. In cell **I20** enter the function **=ERROR.TYPE(H18)** to identify any error in cell **H18**. The result is error type **3**.

10. Close the workbook <u>without</u> saving.

Driving Lesson 31 - Custom Number Formats

Park and Read

As well as formatting cells using the standard number categories such as **Currency** and **Date**, it is possible to create **Custom** formats using a variety of codes. Some of the available codes are listed below:

d	day number without leading zero, e.g. 5
dd	day number with leading zero, e.g. 05
ddd	day abbreviated as text, e.g. Mon
dddd	day as text, e.g. Monday
m	month without leading zero, e.g. 6 (if used after hh *Excel* assumes minutes)
mm	month with leading zero, e.g. 06
mmm	month abbreviated as text, e.g. Jun
mmmm	month as text, e.g. September
h or hh	hours without leading zero based on 24 hour clock unless used with am/pm
[colour]	displays whatever is following in the stated colour Black, Cyan, Magenta, Blue, White, Green, Red and Yellow.
[condition value]	where condition may be <, >, =, >=, <=, <> and value can be any number
#	displays only significant digits
0	displays leading zeros, e.g. 00123
?	adds spaces either side of decimal point
,	thousands separator
.	decimal separator

Driving Lesson 31 - Continued

Manoeuvres

1. Start a new workbook. In cell **B2** enter **56**. Click back on cell **B2** and with the **Home** tab selected, click the **Number** group dialog box launcher, to display the **Format Cells** dialog box.

2. In the **Number** tab, normal formatting is achieved by using the standard categories of **General**, **Number**, **Currency**, **Percentage**, etc. Click **Custom** to display the list from which to select and optionally amend.

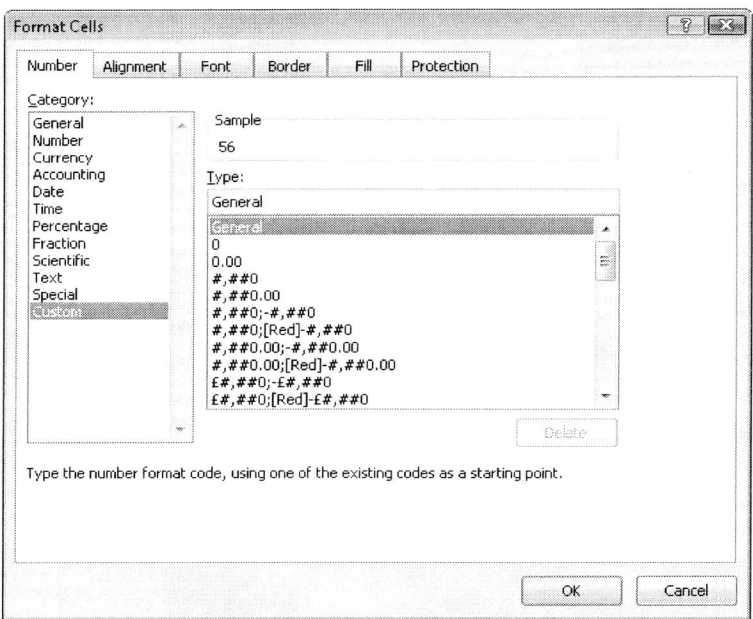

3. The **Type** box is where the custom format is created. Scroll down the list of built-in Types. Select one and check how it affects the display in the **Sample** box.

4. Select the third item in the list **0.00**, edit this in the **Type** box to display just one decimal place, i.e. delete one of the zeros. Click **OK**.

The built-in format used as a starting point for a custom format is still unchanged and available to use.

Driving Lesson 31 - Continued

5. In cell **B4** press **<Ctrl ;>** to enter today's date, press **<Enter>**. Click on cell **B4**, display the **Format Cells** dialog box and click the **Custom** category.

6. To create a custom date, select a date format to work from, choose **dd-mmm-yy**. Edit this in the **Type** box to read **ddd dd mmmm yy**.

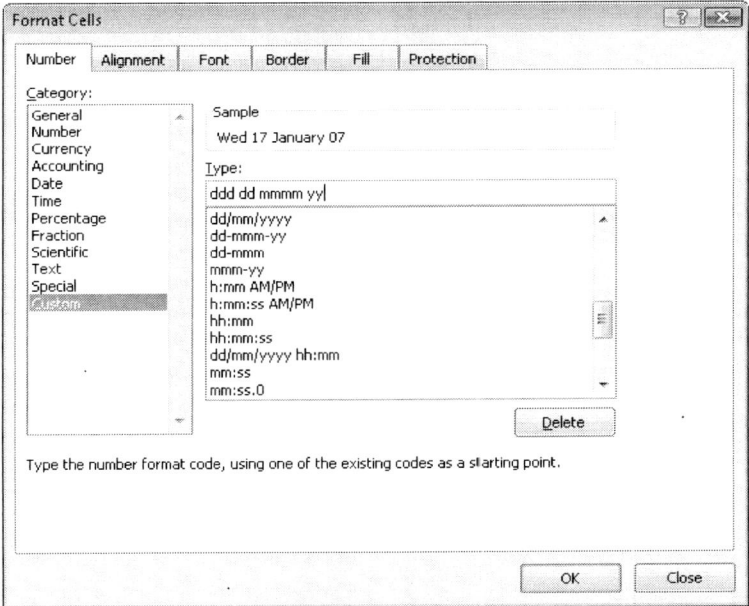

7. Check the **Sample** box and click **OK**. Column **B** is widened to display the date.

8. Enter your birth date in cell **B6** in the form **dd/mm/yyyy**.

9. **Format** this date using the **Custom** date format already created, the **Custom Formats** are stored at the end of the list. This displays the day as well as the date on which you were born.

i   *You may have to widen column **B** to see the date fully displayed.*

10. Close the workbook <u>without</u> saving.

Driving Lesson 32 - S.A.E.

This is not an ECDL test. Testing may only be carried out through certified ECDL test centres. This is a Self-Assessment Exercise. Try to complete it without any reference to the Driving Lessons in this section.

1. Open the workbook **Errors**. This workbook contains a variety of faults, some of which are incorrect ranges in functions that are not shown as errors.

2. Correct any errors that are contained in any of the formulas. For the division by zero error, replace the formulas in that column with an **IF** statement that replaces the error with zero when it occurs.

3. Format the range **J4:K10** with a custom number format to display percentages with one decimal place.

4. In the range **C3:G3** enter the actual dates for last week. Format the range **C3:G3** with custom dates to display a **2** digit day, followed by a **-** then a two digit month, e.g. 03-05 for May 3rd.

5. The range **B4:B9** contains employee numbers. Some contain 3 digits, some 4 and some 5. Custom number format the range so that all the numbers are **6** digits (use the format **000000**) to add the leading zeros.

6. Check cell **K10** it should be **100.0%** if the formulas are correct.

7. Print a copy of the worksheet.

8. Close the worksheet <u>without</u> saving.

i *Check the answers at the back of the guide*

If you experienced any difficulty completing this S.A.E. refer back to the Driving Lessons in this section. Then redo the S.A.E.

Once you are confident with the features, complete the Record of Achievement Matrix referring to the section at the end of the guide. Only when competent move on to the next Section.

Section 8
Scenarios

By the end of this Section you should be able to:

Create Scenarios

Use and Edit Scenarios

Create Scenario Summary Reports

To gain an understanding of the above features, work through the **Driving Lessons** in this **Section**.

For each **Driving Lesson**, read the **Park and Read** instructions, without touching the keyboard, then work through the numbered steps of the **Manoeuvres** on the computer. Complete the **S.A.E.** (Self-Assessment Exercise) at the end of the section to test your knowledge.

Driving Lesson 33 - Creating Scenarios

 Park and Read

When a worksheet is used as a model, certain key input values are varied to see the effect on the resulting solutions. Separate versions of the worksheet, showing different input values and solutions, can be saved as **Scenarios**. This helps in "What-If?" situations, where various solutions can be named and be displayed to compare, for example, the best and worst cases.

Manoeuvres

1. Open the workbook **Food**, which shows the ingredients available to make 3 products and the profit from each product. Varying the production mix for each product (**F5:H5**) will produce different total profit. For the first model ensure that the cells **F5:H5** are all **0**.

2. Highlight the range **F5:H5**. Display the **Data** tab, and from the **Data Tools** group, click ⟦ What-If Analysis ▾ ⟧. Select **Scenario Manager** from the drop down list.

3. In the **Scenario Manager** dialog box, click **Add** then enter the **Scenario** name as **Worst**.

4. Make sure the **Changing cells** are **F5:H5**, then click **OK**.

5. Leave the values of the three changing cells as **0** and click **OK**. **Worst** is now displayed in the **Scenario** list.

6. The next scenario will be a guess to try and maximise the profit. Click **Add**, enter the name as **Guess** and click **OK**.

7. Enter the values of the 3 cells as **100, 120** and **110**.

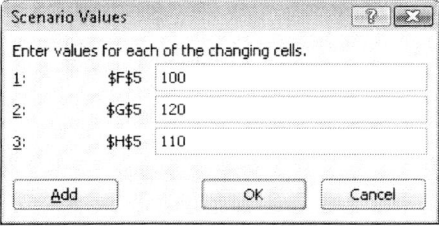

8. Click **OK**.

9. Click **Add** again, enter the name as **Best** and click **OK**. This **Scenario** will use figures that have been calculated elsewhere (using **Solver** - not included in this syllabus) to produce the best possible value of **Profit, G17**. Enter the values of the 3 cells as **159, 167** and **200**, and click **OK**. Click **Close**. Three scenarios have now been created.

10. Save the workbook as **Scenario** and leave the workbook open.

Driving Lesson 34 - Using and Editing Scenarios

▣ Park and Read

Once a set of **Scenarios** have been created, they can be viewed by selecting the required scenario from the list. **Scenarios** can also be edited and deleted using the **Scenario Manager** dialog box.

Manoeuvres

1. The workbook **Scenario** should still be open. If not, open it.

2. Display the **Scenario Manager** from the **What-IF Analysis** drop down. The three scenarios created in the last Driving Lesson are displayed in the list.

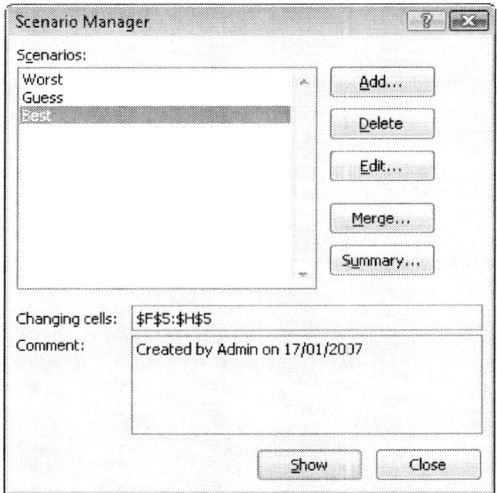

3. Select **Guess** then select **Show** (the dialog box may have to be moved to see the values on the worksheet). The values and the solution for the **Guess** scenario are now displayed.

4. Show the **Best** scenario.

5. Show the **Worst** scenario, click **Edit** and **OK**. The worst scenario can now be changed. Change the values so that they are all **50**. Click on **OK**.

6. Close the **Scenario Manager** dialog box.

7. Save the workbook using the same name and leave it open.

Driving Lesson 35 - Scenario Summary Report

Park and Read

A **Scenario Summary Report** is a report that lists all the scenarios created for a worksheet, along with the **result cells**.

Manoeuvres

1. The workbook **Scenario** should still be open. If not, open it.

2. Display the **Scenario Manager**. Click on **Summary**.

3. The **Result cell** is the **Total Profit**, **G17**. Click on the cell **G17**. Move the dialog box if necessary.

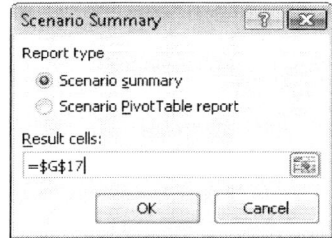

4. Click **OK**. The **Summary Report** is now displayed.

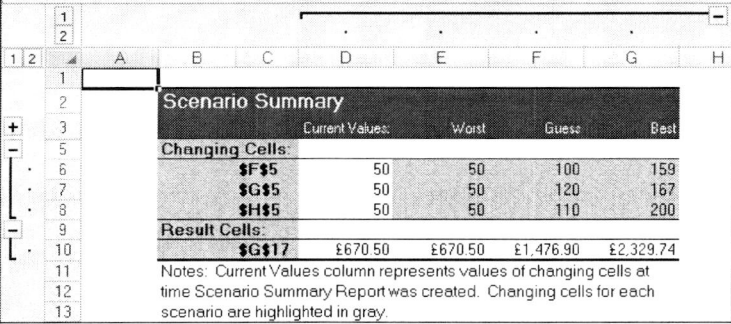

5. The report shows the values of the changing cells and the result cell for each scenario. An **outline view**, is provided, allowing certain rows and columns to be grouped or un-grouped. The outline can be manipulated to change the view of the data. The details of this process are covered in the **Adding Sub Totals** Driving Lesson.

6. The report is created on a separate sheet called **Scenario Summary** within the current workbook.

7. Save the workbook using the same name and then close it.

Driving Lesson 36 - S.A.E.

This is not an ECDL test. Testing may only be carried out through certified ECDL test centres. This is a Self-Assessment Exercise. Try to complete it without any reference to the Driving Lessons in this section.

1. Open the workbook **Mailshot**.

2. The range **C7:C9** should be empty, if not delete the contents of the range.

3. Display the **Scenario Manager** and add the scenario: **Guess1** with the values for **C7:C9** as **800, 700** and **500**.

4. Display the **Scenario Manager** and add the scenario: **Guess2** with the values for **C7:C9** as **1000, 600** and **400**.

5. Display the **Scenario Manager** and add the scenario: **Guess3** with the values for **C7:C9** as **750, 750** and **500**.

6. The three **Scenarios** are now named. Display **Guess2** and print a copy of the worksheet.

7. Use the **Scenario Manager** to produce a **Scenario Summary**, the **Result Cell** is **I11**.

8. Print a copy of the **Scenario Summary**.

9. Use the **Scenario Manager** to delete the Scenario **Guess3**.

10. Save the workbook as **Mailshot Scenarios**.

11. Close the workbook.

If you experienced any difficulty completing this S.A.E. refer back to the Driving Lessons in this section. Then redo the S.A.E.

Once you are confident with the features, complete the Record of Achievement Matrix referring to the section at the end of the guide. Only when competent move on to the next Section.

Section 9
Linking & Importing

By the end of this Section you should be able to:

Link Cells

Link between Worksheets

Link between Workbooks

Link to a Word Document

Exporting Data

Importing Data

Consolidate using 3D-Sum

To gain an understanding of the above features, work through the **Driving Lessons** in this **Section**.

For each **Driving Lesson**, read the **Park and Read** instructions, without touching the keyboard, then work through the numbered steps of the **Manoeuvres** on the computer. Complete the **S.A.E.** (Self-Assessment Exercise) at the end of the section to test your knowledge.

Driving Lesson 37 - Linking

▣ Park and Read

A document link is a formula reference to a cell in the same sheet, another sheet in the same workbook or to another workbook. The sheet that contains the link is called the **container** document. The document pointed to by the link, which has the original data, is known as the **source** document. The reference is **live**, which means that if all sheets are open, any changes in the source document are automatically seen in the container document.

Links can be used to consolidate several related worksheets/workbooks into one. For example, financial information can be collected in separate worksheets from the various divisions within a company, and then gathered together into one workbook to show the overall company results.

To create links between workbooks or other applications, the source application must support **DDE** (Dynamic Data Exchange) or **OLE** (Object Linking and Embedding).

Linking data has a number of advantages:

- To share or consolidate information
- To simplify a complex problem by breaking it down into several separate workbooks
- To divide work among several people
- To build models normally too large for memory
- To add flexibility to workbooks

⌒ Manoeuvres

1. Open the workbook **Link Demo** and select sheet **Consol**. This represents the consolidated results for a company with 3 regions.

2. Click on **C8**. The formula contains a reference to cell **C7** so that if **C7** changes, so will **C8**. This is the simplest form of link.

3. The range **C6** to **F7** contains references like **South!C6**. This is a link referring to the cell **C6** on sheet **South**.

4. Note the profit figure for the **Fourth Quarter** (**-£1282**, i.e. a loss) then switch to the worksheet **South**.

5. Change the value in cell **F6** to **180** and return to the sheet **Consol**. The profit for **Fourth Quarter** has been updated immediately. The profit figure should now be **£7,077**.

ℹ *Links can also be made to cells in different workbooks as described in the* ***Linking Between Workbooks*** *Driving Lesson.*

6. Close the workbook <u>without</u> saving.

Driving Lesson 38 - Creating Links

Park and Read

Links to cells on the same worksheet, as in a formula for example, use the simple cell reference, e.g. **=B3+B4**.

Links created between worksheets differ from cell links in that the reference includes the sheet name followed by a **!** e.g. **=Sheet2!C10**.

To create a **Link** within a workbook, copy and paste from one sheet to another or start entering a formula and point to the required cell/s in other sheets.

Charts are either embedded on the data sheet or placed on a new sheet during the creation process. Charts are linked automatically to the base data.

A 3D-sum function can be used to consolidate data from several worksheets. This is like the normal **Sum** function but instead of adding up a column or along a row, it adds corresponding cells across adjacent worksheets.

Manoeuvres

1. Open the workbook **Links**. This shows sales data from 3 regions on separate sheets and a **Results** sheet on which to consolidate the data. Embedded charts have been created from the data on each of the sheets **North**, **South** and **Mid**. The sales and costs figures for the northern region have been charted on a separate sheet named **Chart**.

2. Click on the **North** worksheet. Charts are linked to the data automatically. Click on cell **D6** and type **5000** and press <Enter>. Note that not only the data changes to match the entry but that the chart is resized to accommodate the new data.

3. Charts created on separate sheets work in the same way. Click on the sheet **Chart**. Note that the **February Sales** are **5000** (and are more than the costs). Click on **North** and return the value in cell **D6** to **3010** by typing or with **Undo**.

4. Check back to **Chart** and note that the **February Sales** figure has changed.

5. Display the **Results** sheet and in cell **C6**, enter the formula **=North!C6+South!C6+Mid!C6,** either by typing or by pointing. This creates links to cell **C6** in each regional sheet to produce a consolidated value.

6. Use the **Fill handle** to copy the formula into **D6** to **F6**. Note that relative addressing is still maintained across the sheets.

7. In **C7** enter the 3D-sum **=SUM(North:Mid!C7)**.

Driving Lesson 38 - Continued

*3D-sum can also be entered using the **AutoSum** button, then selecting the required cell in the **North** sheet, holding down <**Shift**> and clicking the **Mid** sheet tab.*

8.   Copy this formula into **D7** to **F7**.

*To enter links to single cells, **Copy** and **Paste Link** can be used.*

9.   Click cell **H2** in sheet **North** and click the **Copy** button on the **Home** tab in the **Clipboard** group.

10.   Click cell **B3** in sheet **Results**, from the **Paste** drop down select **Paste Link**. This pastes a link to the Manager's name from sheet **North**, not just its current value.

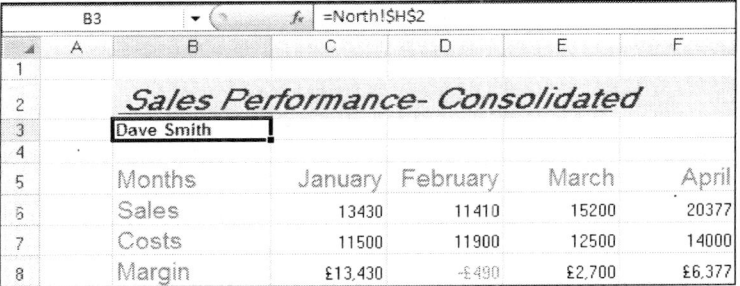

11.   On sheet **North** enter your own name in **H2** as Manager. Switch to sheet **Results** and the name will have been changed.

12.   Change any **Sales** or **Cost** data on the regional sheets and the change will be reflected immediately in the charts and on the **Results** sheet.

13.   Close the workbook <u>without</u> saving.

Driving Lesson 39 - Linking Between Workbooks

Park and Read

Links created between workbooks include the source workbook name as well as the sheet and the cell reference, e.g. **=[budget.xls]Sheet1!C10**. Links are best created with the workbooks open.

If after creating a link the source workbook is closed, then the cell reference formula will also include the full location of the file, e.g.

=C:\...\...Documents\Excel 2007 Data\[budget.xlsx]Sheet1!B7.

To create links between workbooks, copy from the source document and paste into the destination document using the **Paste Link** option.

Charts are simply copied from one workbook and pasted into another.

Always save the source workbook first.

Manoeuvres

1. Open the workbook **Sales**.

2. Click on the chart and copy it.

3. Start a new blank workbook and with the active cell as **A1**, paste the chart. The chart is linked automatically back to **Sales**.

4. In the **Sales** workbook, change the value in cell **C5** to **200000** and note the change in the new workbook.

5. Close both workbooks <u>without</u> saving and start a new blank workbook.

6. In **A1** enter **Source Document**, in cell **B3** enter a number and save the workbook as **Source**.

7. Start a new workbook. In cell **A1** enter **Container Document** and then save it as **Container**.

8. Display the two worksheets side by side by selecting **Arrange All** from the **View** tab. Choose the **Vertical** option and click **OK**.

9. Make **D5** active (point and click) in **Container**.

10. Create a link by typing **=** and make the **Source** workbook active and click on cell **B3**. Press **<Enter>** to complete the formula, which should read:

    =[Source.xlsx]Sheet1!$B$3

11. In **Source**, change the number in cell **B3**. Cell **D5** changes automatically because of the link.

Driving Lesson 39 - Continued

12. Enter a list of 5 numbers starting in **B3** in **Source** down the column. Use the **AutoSum** button to total them in **B8**.

13. In cell **D5** in **Container**, type in the label **Total** to overwrite the earlier link.

14. Make **D6** the active cell in **Container**. Type **=** to start a formula and then point and click on **B8** in the **Source** workbook. Press <**Enter**> to complete the formula. The link is then created and should be;

=[Source.xlsx]Sheet1!$B$8.

*An alternative method of linking is to use **Copy** at the source and then on the container sheet use **Paste Link** button from the **Paste** drop down to create the link.*

15. Copy the contents in cell **B5** in **Source**. Make the workbook **Container** active, click on cell **D8** and create a link, select **Paste Link**.

16. A link has now been created between **B5** in **Source** and **D8** in **Container**. Change the number in **B5**. The numbers in cells **D6** and **D8** in **Container**, and that in **B8** in **Source** change automatically.

17. Save the workbook **Source** and close it.

18. Save the workbook **Container** and close it.

19. Open the workbook **Source**, change two of the numbers in the list and note the total.

20. Save and close the **Source** workbook.

21. Open the **Container** workbook. A message is displayed.

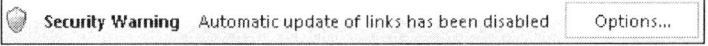

22. The links to **Source** can be updated, click the **Options** button. Select the **Enable this content** option and then click **OK** to update the links. The new total has been retrieved from the unopened workbook.

23. Save and close the workbook **Container**.

Driving Lesson 40 - Linking to a Word Document

▣ Park and Read

A spreadsheet created in *Excel* can be copied into a *Word* document. This can be done in such a way that the data is linked to the workbook it originated from and any changes to the original workbook are reflected in the *Word* document.

☞ Manoeuvres

1. Open the workbook **Sales**. This workbook contains a spreadsheet and a chart, that are to be linked to a word processed document.

2. Start the application *Word*.

3. In a new document, enter the text **This data is linked back to the Sales workbook**.

4. Insert two blank lines (three presses of **<Enter>**), then enter the text **Changes made will be reflected in the document**. Press **<Enter>**.

5. Switch back to the **Sales** workbook in *Excel*.

6. On the **Sales** sheet, select and **copy** the range **B4:E7**.

7. Switch to the document in *Word*. Place the cursor between the two paragraphs.

8. Select **Paste Special** from the **Paste** drop down.

9. In the **Paste Special** dialog box select **Microsoft Office Excel Worksheet Object** from the **As** box. Then select the **Paste link** option.

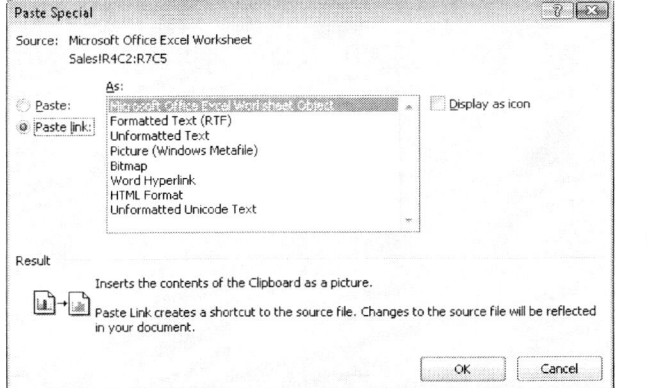

Driving Lesson 40 - Continued

10. Click **OK** to paste the range as a linked object.

11. Switch back to *Excel*, click on the chart and copy it.

12. Switch back to *Word*.

13. Move the cursor to the end of the document and select **Paste Special** from the **Paste** drop down.

14. As before select from the **As** box the **Microsoft Office Excel Chart Object** and select the **Paste link** option. Click **OK**. The chart is linked back to the worksheet.

15. Note the **May** sales for the **North** region is **£150,000**.

16. Save the *Word* document as **Linked** and close it.

17. Switch to *Excel*. Change the **May** sales figure for the **North** to **£130,000** and save the worksheet using the same name.

18. Switch back to *Word* and open the document **Linked**. Click **Yes** to update the links in the document.

This data is linked back to the Sales Workbook

Company Sales	North	Central	South
May	£130,000	£110,743	£90,466
June	£140,376	£100,833	£100,744
July	£140,244	£120,500	£140,775

Changes made will be reflected in the document

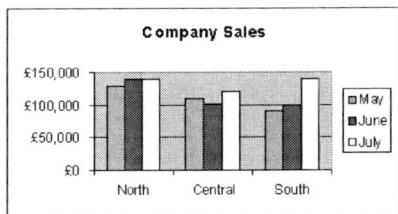

19. The cell in the table and the chart have been updated to show **£130,000**. Save the document and close the *Word* application.

20. In *Excel*, change the **130000** back to **150000**.

21. Save the workbook using the same name and close it.

i   *To make changes to the linked information double click to display the source data in Excel.*

Driving Lesson 41 - Exporting Data

Park and Read

Although the usual format for saving workbooks in *Microsoft Office* is as an **Excel Spreadsheet** (with a **.xlsx** file extension), they can be saved in different formats. One is as a tab delimited **Text** file (with a **.txt** extension). This means that all formulas, formatting, styles and graphics are lost, reducing the cells in a spreadsheet to a series of fixed value fields separated by tabs. The **Comma Delimited** (**.csv**) file is very similar, but the fields are separated by commas. The advantage of these files is that they can be read by almost any application or program, and they are a useful way of transferring raw data.

To save in a format that maintains formulas and most formatting, but can still be read by many different applications, save in **Rich Text Format** (**.rtf** file extension). To enable a spreadsheet to be viewed as a web page, it can be saved in **.htm** format.

The location of saved files can also be specified.

Manoeuvres

1. Open the supplied workbook file **Hotel**. Click the **Office** button and then **Save As**. Change the **File name** to **Hotel2**.

2. Click the **Save as type** box drop down arrow and view the options and their file name extensions. Select **Text (Tab delimited) (*.txt)**.

3. Click **Save**. A dialog box appears warning that only single sheets can be saved in this format. Click **OK**.

4. Another dialog box appears warning that formatting will be lost in this format. Click **Yes**.

5. Select **Save As** again and this time save the file as a **CSV (Comma delimited) (*.csv)** file with a name of **Hotel3**. Click **Save** and then **OK** and **Yes** to the next two messages.

6. Select **Save As** again and this time save the file as a **Web Page (*.htm; *.html)** with a name **Hotel4**. Close the workbook <u>without</u> saving.

7. Open the file **Hotel3.csv** in *Excel*. Ensure **Files of type** displays **All Files**. Notice that all formatting, formulas and links are lost. Close the file.

8. Start the *Windows* application *Notepad*. Open the files **Hotel2.txt** to see how it is stored. Open **Hotel3.csv** (the previous file is automatically closed). Note how this file is stored. Close *Notepad*.

9. View the contents of the folder where the files are saved. Double click on **Hotel4.htm** to open it. It should open in your default web browser application. The content is all present, and most of the formatting is retained. The workbook has 3 worksheets, each displayed as individual web pages, click each page tab to display the different web pages.

10. Close the browser.

Driving Lesson 42 - Importing Data

 Park and Read

Data can be imported to a spreadsheet in various formats.

Data may be imported into a workbook from a text file, as long as the text file has been saved in the correct format and the text set cut in such a manner that separators (tabs, commas, spaces, etc.) can be specified to split the text into the columns.

 Manoeuvres

1. Open the supplied workbook file **Hotel**.

2. Click the **Insert Worksheet** tab, [image] to insert a new worksheet. Rename the sheet **Staff** by double clicking on it.

3. Click in cell **A1** of the **Staff** worksheet then on the **Data** tab. From the **Get External Data** group click, [From Text].

4. Ensure that within **Import Text File**, the folder containing the supplied data is displayed. Ensure that the **Files of type** is set to **All Files**. Select the file **People.csv** from the list and click **Import**.

[i] ***People.csv*** *is a comma delimited data file which could have come from a wide range of sources. If you want to see the structure of it, open it in* ***Notepad***.

5. The **Text Import Wizard** opens. Ensure all options are set as shown. A basic preview of the data layout is shown in the lower part of the box.

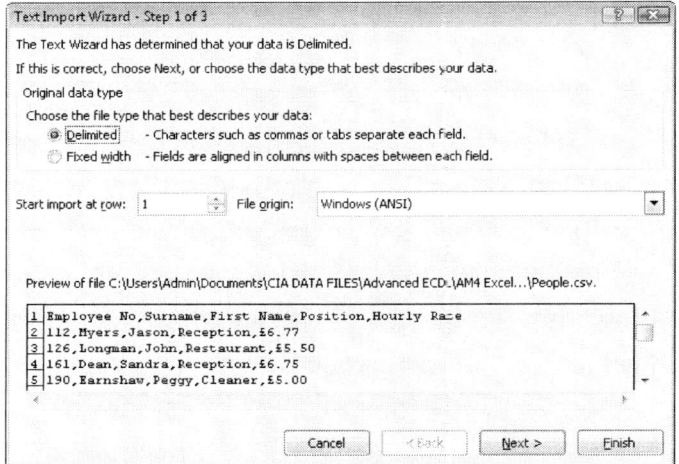

Driving Lesson 42 - Continued

6.　　Click **Next** to display Step 2. Ensure that the **Comma** option is checked in the **Delimiters** section. A clearer preview of the data layout is shown in the lower part of the box.

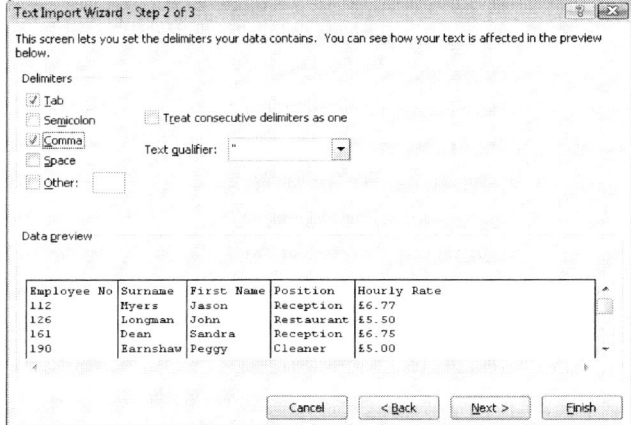

7.　　Click **Next**.

8.　　At Step 3 of 3 format the data in any column by selecting specific columns in the **Data preview** section and setting the required data format in the **Column data format** section. The data in all columns should be set to **General** by default. If not, correct the formats. Click **Finish**.

9.　　The **Import Data** dialog box is displayed.

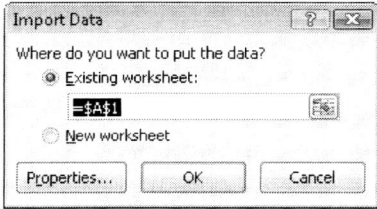

10.　Ensure that the **Existing worksheet** option is checked and the address is **A1**. Click **OK**. The data from the text file **People.csv** is imported into the empty worksheet, starting at cell **A1**.

11.　Close the workbook without saving.

Driving Lesson 43 - S.A.E.

This is not an ECDL test. Testing may only be carried out through certified ECDL test centres. This is a Self-Assessment Exercise. Try to complete it without any reference to the Driving Lessons in this section.

1. Make sure that there are no workbooks open, even a blank workbook. Open the workbooks **Hotel03**, **Hotel04**, and **Hotel05**.

2. The occupancy figures for single rooms are to be compared over the three year period. Open **Hotel Library**.

3. The single room bookings are all stored in **B7:M7** of the 3 source workbooks. The ranges to copy have all been named **singles**. Create the necessary links to **Hotel Library**.

4. Make **Hotel Library** active and maximise the window. Enter the formulas to calculate % occupancy in the rows **10** to **12**, assume a **300** room per month capacity (rooms/300).

5. Format the range **B10:M12** as percentages to two decimal places.

6. Sum in cell **N6** all the monthly figures. Copy the formula to cells **N7** and **N8**.

7. Enter a function to average the monthly occupancy figures in cell **N10**. Copy the formula to cells **N11** and **N12**.

8. Use **Page Layout** and **Print Preview** to set the worksheet to print on one piece of paper, landscape. Print a copy of the worksheet.

9. Save the workbook as **Hotel Occupancy**.

10. Chart the occupancy rows as a three series **Line** chart (remember to include the month labels). Move the chart to a separate sheet.

11. Print a copy of the chart.

12. Close all the open workbooks <u>without</u> saving.

 A copy of the completed chart is included in the answers at the back of the guide.

If you experienced any difficulty completing this S.A.E. refer back to the Driving Lessons in this section. Then redo the S.A.E.

Once you are confident with the features, complete the Record of Achievement Matrix referring to the section at the end of the guide. Only when competent move on to the next Section.

Section 10
Sorting

By the end of this Section you should be able to:

Sort Data

Perform Multiple Sorts

Customise Sorts

To gain an understanding of the above features, work through the **Driving Lessons** in this **Section**.

For each **Driving Lesson**, read the **Park and Read** instructions, without touching the keyboard, then work through the numbered steps of the **Manoeuvres** on the computer. Complete the **S.A.E.** (Self-Assessment Exercise) at the end of the section to test your knowledge.

Driving Lesson 44 - Sorting

Park and Read

Ranges of cells in a worksheet can be sorted so that the rows in the range are arranged in a specific order. The column used to control the sort is called the **Sort Key**.

Manoeuvres

1. Start a new blank workbook.

2. Enter a column of 8 names (surnames or first names) starting in cell **B3**.

3. Sort the names into ascending alphabetic order by highlighting the range to be sorted (**B3:B10**) and from the **Home** tab, **Editing** group, click **Sort & Filter** and select **Sort A to Z**.

> ℹ️ *Selecting the whole range to be sorted is not strictly necessary in this example but this shows the technique of sorting cells that may be part of a larger worksheet.*

4. With the range still selected, sort the range in descending order using **Sort Z to A**.

5. Add ages (in years) in column **C** adjacent to the names.

6. To sort all of the data in ascending order of age, highlight the range **B3:C10** and select **Custom Sort** from the **Sort & Filter** drop down.

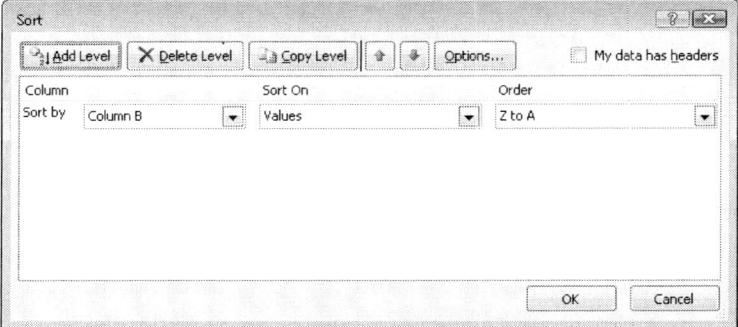

7. Select **Column C** from **Sort by**, **Smallest to Largest** from **Order** and click **OK** to perform the sort.

8. Close the workbook <u>without</u> saving.

Driving Lesson 45 - Multiple Column Sorts

Park and Read

In a list, the records (rows) can be sorted into a specific order based on the values of one or more of the fields (columns).

To sort a list, the method is the same as for an ordinary sort, except that the data does not have to be selected prior to sorting, selecting a cell anywhere in the list will automatically sort the whole list.

Manoeuvres

1.　In a new workbook, enter the list information as shown in the rows and columns below, i.e. starting in cell **A6**.

	A	B	C	D	E	F	G
6	Make	Model	Reg.No	Engine	Colour	Mileage	Price
7	Austin	Maestro	YK51 LMT	1600	Silver Grey	7124	2250
8	Vauxhall	Corsa	Y19 LTJ	1300	Black	74123	1250

2.　Open the workbook **Car Data**.

3.　To add more data to the list, **copy** the range **A1:G10** in **Car Data** to a range starting **A9** in the workbook opened at step 1.

4.　Save the workbook as **Cars**.

5.　Close the **Car Data** workbook.

6.　Select **Custom Sort** from the **Sort & Filter** drop down to display the **Sort** dialog box.

7.　Check the **My data has headers** box.

8.　Sort the list into ascending order by **Make**.

9.　Click **Add Level** to perform a secondary sort in ascending order by **Model**.

10.　The list is defined as having a header row with **Make** in the **Sort by** box and **Model** in the first **Then by** box.

Driving Lesson 45 - Continued

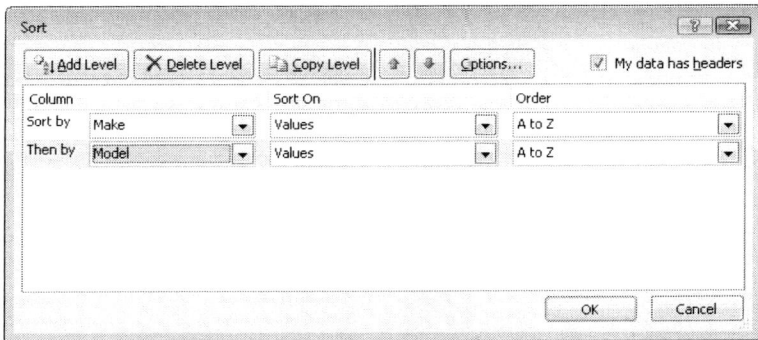

11. Click **OK** to perform the sort.

12. Use the **Undo** button on the **Quick Access Toolbar** to return the list to the original order.

13. Insert a new **Column A** and set the column width to **3.00** units.

14. Label the column **No** and enter **1** in cell **A7**.

15. Select the range **A7:A18**. Using the **Home** tab, click **Fill**, from the **Editing** group. Click to select **Series** and then click **OK**, to number each row, in order, starting with 1 up to 12.

16. Sort by **Price** in descending order. Which car is the second cheapest?

17. Sort the cars into ascending numeric order by **Mileage**. Which car has the most mileage?

18. Using column **A** re-sort the range back to its original order.

> **i** *If records are to be returned to their original order after sorting, leading zeros may have to be added to labels that include numbers so that they sort correctly.*

19. Save the workbook using the same file name.

20. Close the workbook.

> **i** *Check the answers at the back of the guide*

Driving Lesson 46 - Custom Sorts

Park and Read

The normal **Sort** function will order items alphabetically or numerically, ascending or descending. It is however possible to sort data into any specified order using **Custom Lists**. Some **Custom Lists** are provided as defaults in *Excel*, others can be defined by the user.

Manoeuvres

1. Open the workbook **Invoices**.

2. Type **Order Day** in cell **H5**, and **Tuesday** in cell **H6**.

3. Enter a random selection of days of the week into cells **H7** to **H14.** to represent the day on which each order was received. As this is a demonstration only, do not worry about matching days to the date field.

4. A normal sort on the **Order Day** column will arrange the days in alphabetical order. To sort into weekday order, click a cell in column **H** and select **Sort & Filter** then **Custom Sort**.

5. Make sure the **Sort by** box shows **Order Day** and click the **Order** drop down list and select **Custom List**.

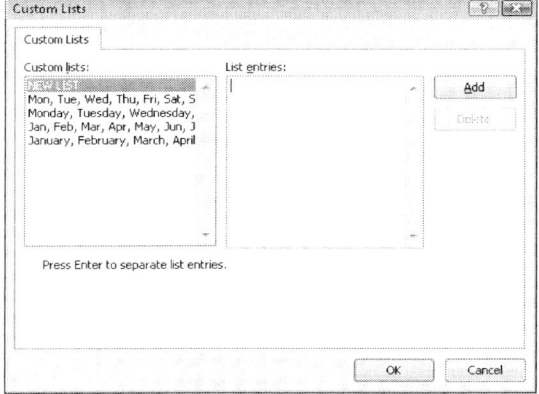

6. Select the list starting **Monday, Tuesday** and click **OK** to return to the **Sort** dialog box.

7. Click **OK** to sort the list into weekday order.

 *User defined **Custom Lists** can be created using the Custom Lists dialog box, click **NEW LIST**, enter a list, use <**Enter**> after each item then click **Add**.*

8. Close the workbook <u>without</u> saving.

Driving Lesson 47 - S.A.E.

This is not an ECDL test. Testing may only be carried out through certified ECDL test centres. This is a Self-Assessment Exercise. Try to complete it without any reference to the Driving Lessons in this section.

1.　Open the workbook **League**.

2.　Sort the teams into alphabetic name order.

3.　**Undo** the last operation.

4.　Sort the teams into descending order of points. If the points are equal, then sort on the goal difference, again in descending order. Then sort on the number of goals-for (descending).

5.　Print a copy of the league table.

6.　Close the workbook <u>without</u> saving.

7.　Open the workbook **Supplies** showing part of the order book for a Building Supplies Merchant.

8.　Using a **Custom Sort**, sort the records first by **Month Required** but in the order of **Jan**, **Feb**, etc. and then by ascending **Customer** name.

9.　Print a copy of the worksheet.

10.　Close the workbook <u>without</u> saving.

If you experienced any difficulty completing this S.A.E. refer back to the Driving Lessons in this section. Then redo the S.A.E.

Once you are confident with the features, complete the Record of Achievement Matrix referring to the section at the end of the guide. Only when competent move on to the next Section.

Section 11
Lists

By the end of this Section you should be able to:

Create a List

Filter Lists using the AutoFilter

Use Custom Criteria with AutoFilter

Use the Advanced Filter

Filter using Complex Criteria

Extract Filtered Data

Add Subtotals

To gain an understanding of the above features, work through the **Driving Lessons** in this **Section**.

For each **Driving Lesson**, read the **Park and Read** instructions, without touching the keyboard, then work through the numbered steps of the **Manoeuvres** on the computer. Complete the **S.A.E.** (Self-Assessment Exercise) at the end of the section to test your knowledge.

Driving Lesson 48 - Lists

Park and Read

A **List** is a labelled series of rows that contain similar information - for example a list of employees, showing their names, salaries, expenses, holidays, etc. A list can be used to:

- Search or query to find specific data.

- Sort data alphabetically or numerically by rows in ascending or descending order.

- Search for matching criteria by filtering and copy to a different part of the spreadsheet.

- Perform statistical calculations on the data for analysis and decision-making.

- Print data organised for specific purposes.

A **List** separates information into columns, each containing similar information. A row contains a set of **fields**, each defined by **field names**. A completed row is a **record**. A list is composed of many such records. The field names appear as column headings with the field information below them.

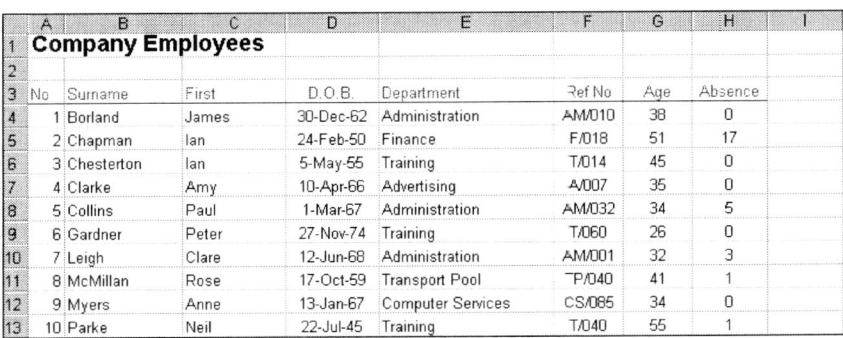

	A	B	C	D	E	F	G	H	I
1	**Company Employees**								
2									
3	No	Surname	First	D.O.B.	Department	Ref No	Age	Absence	
4	1	Borland	James	30-Dec-62	Administration	AM/010	38	0	
5	2	Chapman	Ian	24-Feb-50	Finance	F/018	51	17	
6	3	Chesterton	Ian	5-May-55	Training	T/014	45	0	
7	4	Clarke	Amy	10-Apr-66	Advertising	A/007	35	0	
8	5	Collins	Paul	1-Mar-67	Administration	AM/032	34	5	
9	6	Gardner	Peter	27-Nov-74	Training	T/060	26	0	
10	7	Leigh	Clare	12-Jun-68	Administration	AM/001	32	3	
11	8	McMillan	Rose	17-Oct-59	Transport Pool	TP/040	41	1	
12	9	Myers	Anne	13-Jan-67	Computer Services	CS/085	34	0	
13	10	Parke	Neil	22-Jul-45	Training	T/040	55	1	

A sample list occupying the range A3:H13

A field containing formulas or functions is called a computed field.

> *Avoid having more than one list on each worksheet. Filtering can only be used on one list at a time. The column labels at the top of a list can use two rows providing the labels are formatted differently to the list, e.g. font, alignment, colour, patterns, etc.*

Driving Lesson 49 - Creating a List

▣ Park and Read

Enter the **Column** names (**Fields**) as labels across a row. The data is entered directly below them, following these rules:

- The area to be used must be rectangular, although it may contain blanks.

- Use the same type of data in each column.

- Do not separate the labels from the data with a blank or decorative row.

- Do not duplicate column names and to avoid confusion they should be different from any range names.

- Enter all the list information across each row.

☞ Manoeuvres

1. In a new workbook, enter the list information as shown in the rows and columns below, adjusting the column widths as necessary:

	A	B	C	D	E
1					
2					
3	Item	Classification	Price	Sold Today?	
4	Full Fat Milk	Dairy	0.89	Yes	
5	Butter	Dairy	0.95	Yes	
6	Basmati Rice	Provisions	1.39	Yes	
7	Cauliflower	Fruit and Veg	0.25	Yes	
8	Pizza	Frozen	2.99	Yes	
9	Country Ham	Delicatessen	0.75	Yes	
10	Gorgonzola	Delicatessen	1.75	Yes	
11	Semi-Skimmed Milk	Dairy	0.89	Yes	
12	Guinness	Wines and Spirits	4.95	Yes	
13	Weetabix (24)	Provisions	1.26	Yes	
14	Crisps (6)	Provisions	0.99	Yes	
15	Coffee	Provisions	2.45	Yes	
16	Bananas	Fruit and Veg	1.29	Yes	
17	Beaujolais	Wines and Spirits	3.25	Yes	
18	Yogurt	Dairy	1.25	Yes	
19					

2. Save the workbook as **Corner shop**. As the data has been entered in list format, it could now be filtered as shown in the following Driving Lessons.

3. Close the workbook.

Driving Lesson 50 - Filtering Lists

▣ Park and Read

Filtering is a quick way to find records in a list that match search criteria. Only the rows that match are displayed. The rows that do not match are hidden, not deleted.

There are two ways to filter a list: the **AutoFilter** (for a simple filter) and the **Advanced Filter** (for more complex filtering). When a list is filtered, the worksheet is placed in **Filter Mode**.

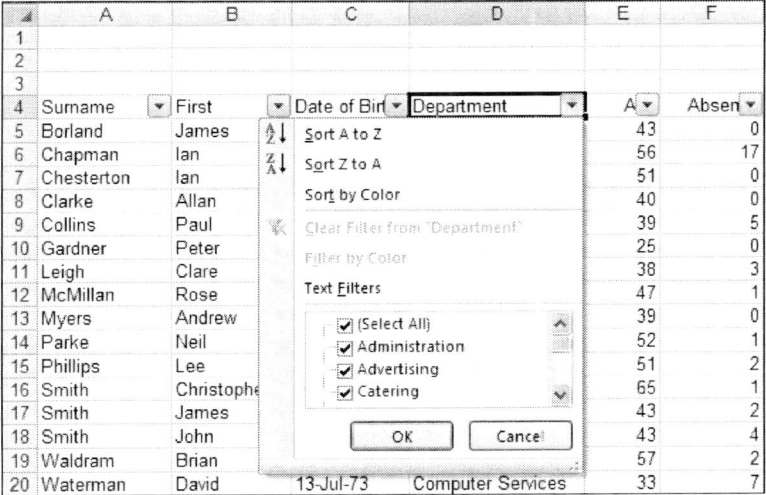

*A worksheet in **Filter Mode***

In **Filter Mode**, the labels at the top of the list columns contain drop down arrows. If one of these arrows is clicked, a list of all different values in the column is revealed. The filter to be applied can then be selected from the list.

The default view is to show all rows **(Select All)**, until an alternative selection is made from the **Text Filters** list. Other options include:

Sort A to Z	to sort the list into ascending order
Sort Z to A	to sort the list into descending order
Sort by Color	where criteria can be applied and data can be compared via **Custom Sort**.

In the example above, all members of staff in the **Catering** department can be displayed by un-checking **(Select All)** and checking **Catering** from the drop down list for **Department**.

Driving Lesson 51 - AutoFilter

Park and Read

AutoFilter produces a subset of a list with the click of a button. This places the worksheet in **Filter Mode**. Click on any of the arrows to display a drop down list of unique values in that column. Click on any item and the matching records (rows) will be displayed with the other rows hidden.

AutoFilter always selects from the whole list. **AutoFilter** can be applied to selected columns in a list by selecting them before entering **Filter Mode**.

Manoeuvres

1. Open the workbook **Sick**.

2. Enter **Filter Mode** by clicking on a cell in the list and then in the **Data** tab, within the **Sort & Filter** group, click the **Filter** button, 〈Filter〉.

3. Using the **Surname** drop down list, scroll down the list, un-check **Select All**, check **Smith** and click **OK**. Only the Smiths are displayed.

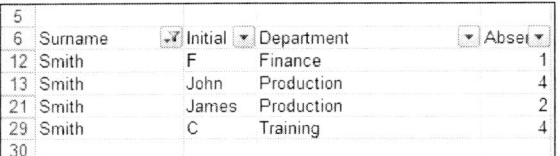

	Surname	Initial	Department	Abse
5				
6	Surname	Initial	Department	Abse
12	Smith	F	Finance	1
13	Smith	John	Production	4
21	Smith	James	Production	2
29	Smith	C	Training	4
30				

The drop down arrows are displayed as, ⌁, if active with a filter applied.

4. To redisplay the full list using the **Surname** drop down list, check **(Select All)** at the top of the list and click **OK**.

5. Exit **Filter Mode** by selecting the **Filter** button again.

6. Open the workbook **Survey** and click on any cell in the list.

7. Enter **Filter Mode**.

8. To display all the males from Sunderland who have replied, select **M** from **Sex**, **Sunderland** from **Town** and **1** from **Reply**.

9. To redisplay the whole list, instead of checking **Select All** from the three lists, click **Clear**, ⌁ Clear in the **Sort & Filter** group. All filter selections are removed.

A filtered list can be printed.

10. Click **Filter** to exit **Filter Mode**.

11. Close the workbook **Survey** without saving and leave the workbook **Sick** open.

Driving Lesson 52 - Custom AutoFilter

 Park and Read

Custom AutoFilter allows more complicated details than a simple information match. Two conditions for selecting values within the same column can be applied by using any of the 12 options (equals, is less than, etc.). **Custom AutoFilters** can be applied both to **numbers** and **text** columns.

 Manoeuvres

1. The workbook **Sick** should still be open. If not, open it.

2. Using the workbook **Sick**, enter filter mode by clicking on a cell in the list and then in the **Data** tab, within the **Sort & Filter** group, click the **Filter** button.

3. Click on the **Absent** drop down list and select **Number Filters**.

*Simple searches can be carried out using one set of criteria. More complicated filters can be carried out using either **And** or **Or** to then add another set of criteria.*

4. To display all the employees who have had less than five days absence, select **Less Than** from the list. The **Custom AutoFilter** dialog box is displayed. Enter **5** in the **Information** box.

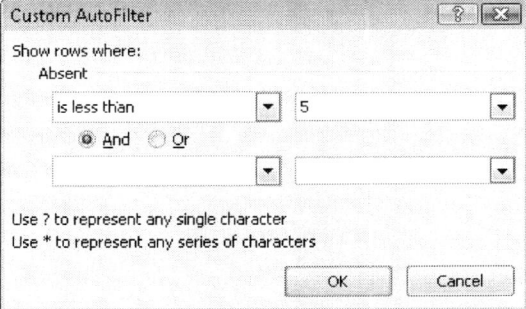

5. Click **OK**. The drop down of **Absent** is displayed as, , showing that a filter has been applied.

6. To restore the list, click on the **Absent** field drop down list and check **Select All** and click **OK**.

7. To display all the employees in either the **Administration** or **Computer Services** departments using **Custom AutoFilter**, click on the **Department** field drop down list and select **Text Filters**.

Driving Lesson 52 - Continued

8.　Select **Equals**.

9.　Use the drop down **Information** box to select **Administration**.

10.　Select the **Or** option.

11.　Select **equals** from the first drop down list and **Computer Services** from the second.

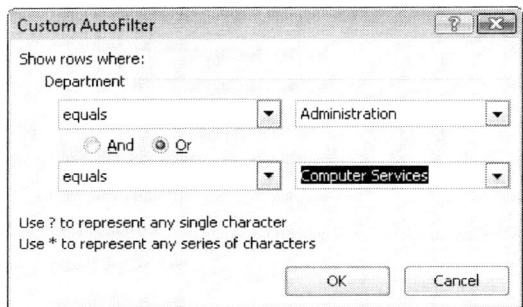

12.　Click **OK** to complete the filter.

13.　Exit **Filter Mode** by clicking the **Filter** button.

14.　Leave the workbook **Sick** open for the next Driving Lesson.

Driving Lesson 53 - Advanced Filtering

Park and Read

To search a list for more complex criteria, e.g. matching information from two fields rather than one, **Advanced Filter** can be used. This involves setting up a **Criteria Range** in a separate range of cells, normally to the top or right of the list. The **Criteria Range** consists of at least 2 rows, the column headings for the list, and one or more rows directly underneath to enter the **selection criteria**. Once this has been set up, then the list can be filtered.

A **Criteria Range** can also be arranged to combine two searches by placing information on the same row (combination '**and**') or on two rows (combination '**or**'). If the same name is required for an 'and' combination the field name must be duplicated.

Manoeuvres

1. Open the workbook **Sick**, if not already open.

2. To create a criteria range, copy the field names **A6:D6** to row 1 (**Copy** is found on the **Home** tab or right click for a shortcut menu).

 Copying the field names results in fewer mistakes being made than by typing. Also copying all the names means that other filters can be performed using the same range.

3. To setup a search for all the staff in administration with less than 5 days absence, on row **2** enter **Administration** under **Department** and **<5** under **Absent**.

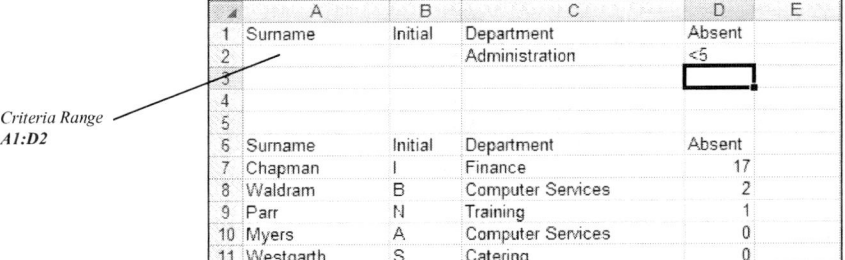

Criteria Range A1:D2

	A	B	C	D	E
1	Surname	Initial	Department	Absent	
2			Administration	<5	
3					
4					
5					
6	Surname	Initial	Department	Absent	
7	Chapman	I	Finance	17	
8	Waldram	B	Computer Services	2	
9	Parr	N	Training	1	
10	Myers	A	Computer Services	0	
11	Westgarth	S	Catering	0	

 The criteria range must be at least one column and two rows. The first row contains the field names in any order. The other rows contain the required selection criteria for the filter.

4. The criteria range is now set up for the filtering to take place. Select a cell in the main list and in the **Data** tab, click the **Advanced** button, from the **Sort & Filter** group.

Driving Lesson 53 - Continued

5.   The **List range** has been automatically defined and is correct. Click in the **Criteria range** box and select the range **A1:D2** (it could have been **C1:D2**, as this is all that is being used but using the larger range means that other filtering can be done later with other fields without redefining the criteria range).

6.   Leave the other options as they are and click **OK** to filter the list in-place.

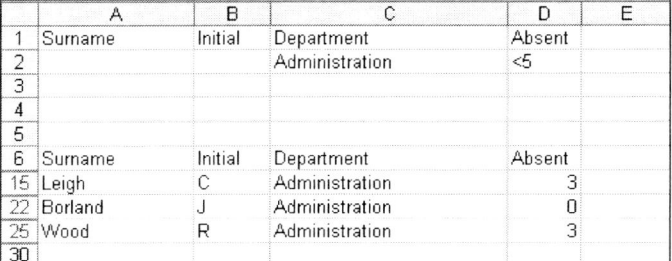

7.   Return to the full list using the **Clear** button, ▼ Clear.

8.   Try another **'and'** filter by clearing row **2** and entering new search criteria.

9.   Close the workbook <u>without</u> saving.

10.   Open the workbook **Invoices**.

11.   To filter the list using the **Invoice** and **Amount** fields, copy those two field names from row **5** to row **A1** and **B1** to set up the **Criteria Range**.

Driving Lesson 53 - Continued

12. To find invoice numbers less than 170 and amounts of more than £1000 excluding Vat., enter **<170** below **Invoice** and **>1000** below **Amount**.

	A	B	C
1	Invoice	Amount	
2	<170	>1000	
3			

13. Select a cell in the list and click the **Advanced** button.

14. Click in the **Criteria Range** box and select the range **A1:B2** on the worksheet. Click **OK** to filter the list.

	Invoice	Date	Co. No.	Company	Amount	VAT	Total
5	Invoice	Date	Co. No.	Company	Amount	VAT	Total
8	167	21-Dec-03	345	J Jones	£1,345.00	£235.38	£1,580.38

15. There should only be one record. Click the **Clear** button to remove the filter.

16. The last example was of an 'and' search. To find the invoices dated before 1st Jan 2004 or totals over 750, an 'or' search is needed. Delete the range **A1:B2** and create the following criteria range:

	A	B
1	Date	Total
2	<1/1/04	
3		>750

17. Using **Advanced Filter** and the **Criteria Range** as **A1:B3** (to include the extra row) display the matching records (there should be **6**).

18. Click on a cell in the list and click **Clear**.

19. Delete the data from the range **A1:B3**.

20. A more difficult search would involve, for example, **Amounts** between £300 and £500 (note these values exclude VAT). This is an **and** search (on the same line) but the field name has to be given twice. Create the criteria range as shown right. (**AutoFilter** can do the same task and is easier).

	A	B
1	Amount	Amount
2	>300	<500

21. Use the **Advanced Filter** to display the matching records.

	Invoice	Date	Co. No.	Company	Amount	VAT	Total
5	Invoice	Date	Co. No.	Company	Amount	VAT	Total
6	156	3-Dec-03	378	Greens	£456.00	£79.80	£535.80
9	168	21-Dec-03	387	CIA Training Ltd	£345.50	£60.46	£405.96
14	176	13-Jan-04	198	Car Mart	£378.00	£66.15	£444.15

22. Remove the filter.

23. Delete the data from the range **A1:B2**.

24. Leave the workbook **Invoices** open for the next Driving Lesson.

Driving Lesson 54 - Extracting Filtered Data

Park and Read

Extracting means copying the filtered records that match the criteria to another part of the worksheet. All the field names need not be used, so that specific information for a specific purpose can be extracted to form another list. The original list remains unaffected.

Manoeuvres

1. The workbook **Invoices** should still be open. If not, open it.

2. Copy the range **A5:G5** and paste to cell **A1**. In cell **G2** enter **<1000** to find all the small amounts owed.

3. Select a cell in the list and display the **Data** tab. Click the **Advanced** button from the **Sort & Filter** group.

4. Select **A1:G2** as the **Criteria range**.

5. Select the **Copy to another location** option.

6. Click in the **Copy to** box and then click on cell **A20**.

7. Click **OK**. The matching records are placed in a range starting **A20**.

8. Delete the range **A20:G25**.

9. Only a part of the list is to be extracted: **Invoice**, **Company** and **Total**. Copy the three field names one at a time to the range **A20:C20**.

10. Select a cell in the list then select the **Advanced Filter**, **Copy to another location** and in the **Copy to** box add the range **A20:C20**.

11. Click **OK** to extract the matching records. Only fields for the selected headers are extracted.

12. Close the workbook <u>without</u> saving.

Driving Lesson 55 - Adding SubTotals

 Park and Read

Data in a **List** can be automatically summarised, producing subtotals based on any column. The list must first be sorted on the column for which subtotals are required. **Subtotals** are then automatically inserted on each break within that column, as well as a **Grand Total** for the whole column. Although the **SUM** function is usually used in subtotals, other functions such as **COUNT** or **AVERAGE** can be used.

When subtotals are added an **Outline View** of the list is produced grouping the data rows. This outline can be manipulated, for example to hide the detail rows and show only the subtotals.

Manoeuvres

1. Open the workbook **Sick**.

2. To display a total for the days absent, subtotalled by **Department**, first sort the list by column **C**, the **Department** column.

3. Select a cell in the list and then in the **Data** tab, **Outline** group, select **Subtotal** to display the **Subtotal** dialog box.

4. Click in the **At each change in:** box and select **Department**.

5. Click in the **Use function:** box to see the possible options, but leave it set to **Sum**.

6. Make sure that in **Add subtotal to:** there is a check in the **Absent** box.

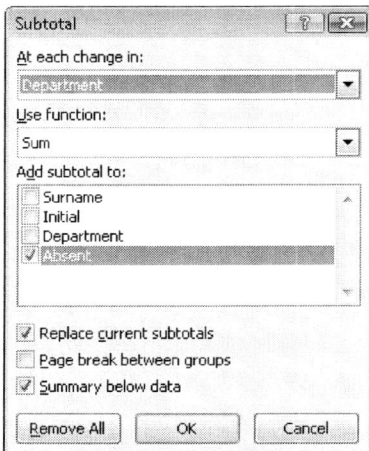

Driving Lesson 55 - Continued

7. Leave the other options as shown and click **OK**. The list is now displayed with **Absent** subtotals for each **Department**, a **Grand Total** at the end, and an **Outline view** of the list to the left of the worksheet area.

8. The **Outline** view shows that there are three levels in this list, **1**=**Grand Total**, **2**=**Department** subtotal, **3**=full detail. By default all levels are displayed on the worksheet. Click on the **Level 2** button at the top of the outline view to collapse level 3 and only show subtotals.

9. Click on the **Level 1** button to collapse subtotals and only show the grand total. Individual groups may be collapsed and expanded by clicking their **Hide** buttons ⊟, or **Show** buttons ⊞.

10. Click the **Show** button ⊞, for the **Grand Total** to expand back to subtotals. Click the **Show** button for the **Production Total** to expand that group only.

11. Click the **Level 3** button to expand all levels again.

12. To remove the **Subtotals** select **Subtotal** from the **Outline** group on the **Data** tab and click the **Remove All** button.

13. Close the workbook <u>without</u> saving.

Driving Lesson 56 - S.A.E.

This is not an ECDL test. Testing may only be carried out through certified ECDL test centres. This is a Self-Assessment Exercise. Try to complete it without any reference to the Driving Lessons in this section.

1.   Open the workbook **Staff**.

2.   Display the **AutoFilter** and filter the list to display only the employees in the **Computer Services** department.

3.   Display all the records.

4.   Filter the list to show the employees between **40** and **50** years old inclusive.

5.   Remove the **AutoFilter**.

6.   Insert **3** more rows under row **1**.

7.   Copy the field names to row **3**.

8.   Use the **Advanced Filter** to extract a record of the employees in the **Administration** department, starting at cell **A30**.

9.   Print a copy of the workbook.

10. Close the workbook <u>without</u> saving.

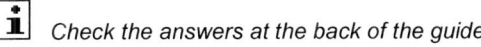 *Check the answers at the back of the guide*

If you experienced any difficulty completing this S.A.E. refer back to the Driving Lessons in this section. Then redo the S.A.E.

Once you are confident with the features, complete the Record of Achievement Matrix referring to the section at the end of the guide. Only when competent move on to the next Section.

Section 12
Pivot Tables

By the end of this Section you should be able to:

Understand PivotTables

Create a PivotTable

Update a PivotTable

Group Data in a PivotTable

To gain an understanding of the above features, work through the **Driving Lessons** in this **Section**.

For each **Driving Lesson**, read the **Park and Read** instructions, without touching the keyboard, then work through the numbered steps of the **Manoeuvres** on the computer. Complete the **S.A.E.** (Self-Assessment Exercise) at the end of the section to test your knowledge.

Driving Lesson 57 - Pivot Tables

Park and Read

A **PivotTable** organises and then summarises large amounts of data from any range that has labelled columns. Typically, two of the fields from the original data can act as the row and column headings for the new table. A third can optionally be used to group the tables into separate pages. **PivotTables** are created by default on a separate worksheet but can be created on the same sheet by entering a starting cell reference that does not clash with the original base data.

Manoeuvres

1. Open the workbook **Survey**.

2. Click inside the list and select in the **Insert** tab, **Tables** group, **PivotTable**.

3. The **Create PivotTable** dialog box is displayed. The **Table/Range** is selected correctly. The **PivotTable** is to be created on a **New Worksheet**. Click **OK**.

4. A blank **PivotTable** is placed on a new sheet with the **PivotTable Field List** displayed.

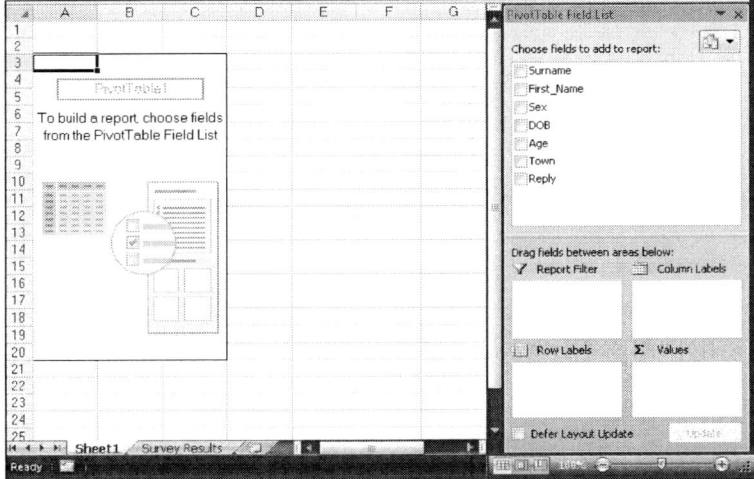

Driving Lesson 57 - Continued

5. **Fields** are checked from the **PivotTable Field List**, on to PivotTable areas. Drag **Town** to the **Row Labels** section and **Sex** to the **Column Labels** section.

6. To summarise data into area by the sex of the people in the survey, drag the **Town** field on to the **Values** area. The default calculation for text fields is **Count**.

3	Count of Town	Column Labels ▼		
4	Row Labels ▼	F	M	Grand Total
5	Bristol		2	2
6	Carlisle		1	1
7	Durham	16	17	33
8	Newcastle	17	26	43
9	South Shields	12	12	24
10	Sunderland	28	35	63
11	Tynemouth	1	2	3
12	Washington	22	29	51
13	**Grand Total**	**96**	**124**	**220**

7. The **PivotTable** is created. Click on the sheet away from the **PivotTable**; the **PivotTable Field List** is hidden. Click inside the **PivotTable** and the **PivotTable Field List** is re-displayed.

8. To organise the table differently the fields can be changed round, i.e. pivoted. Change **Town** and **Sex** over by dragging the buttons to each others area. Observe the changes then return **Town** and **Sex** to their original positions.

9. Go back to the **Survey Results** sheet and make some changes to **Town** fields (people have moved house).

10. The **PivotTable** is now out of date, click on **Sheet1**, the sheet containing the PivotTable and then click inside the table. **PivotTables** do not automatically update, under **PivotTable Tools**, in the **Options** tab, **Data** group, click the **Refresh** button.

[i] *An alternative method to update a **PivotTable** is with the active cell inside the table, right click and select **Refresh**.*

11. Save the workbook as **Survey2**.

12. Leave the workbook **Survey2** open for the next Driving Lesson.

Driving Lesson 58 - Grouping Data in Pivot Tables

Park and Read

As well as displaying data summarised by any of the columns in the original list, **Pivot Tables** can be also be used to further arrange items into new groups. For example, with data summarised by month, January, February and March can be further grouped into Quarter1; or with data grouped by town, selected towns can be grouped to form Region 1.

Once data has been grouped, the original detail can be hidden so that only the group totals are shown.

Manoeuvres

1. If the workbook **Survey2** is not open, open it now and select the sheet containing the Pivot Table. The object will be to group the town data into regions.

2. Select the **Options** tab. From the **Show/Hide** group, click **Field Headers** to remove the row and column labels.

3. Click to select **Durham**, hold down the <**Ctrl**> key, and click on **Sunderland** and **Washington** in Column **A**, then release <**Ctrl**>.

4. Click the **Group Selection** button in the **Group** group to create a group containing those towns.

5. The group will be named **Group1** by default. Click on the name and change it to **Wearside**.

6. Define another group containing **Newcastle**, **South Shields** and **Tynemouth** and call it **Tyneside**.

7. Select any remaining towns and group them under the name **Other**.

	Count of Town			
3				
4		F	M	Grand Total
5	⊟ **Other**			
6	Bristol		2	2
7	Carlisle		1	1
8	⊟ **Wearside**			
9	Durham	16	17	33
10	Sunderland	28	35	63
11	Washington	22	29	51
12	⊟ **Tyneside**			
13	Newcastle	17	26	43
14	South Shields	12	12	24
15	Tynemouth	1	2	3
16	**Grand Total**	**96**	**124**	**220**

Driving Lesson 58 - Continued

 *Fields can also be grouped by right clicking any of the highlighted fields and selecting **Group**.*

8. The title for the new group column has defaulted to **Town2** (being a grouping of Towns). Click on one of the group names and select **Field Settings** on the **Options** tab. Change the name to **Region**. Click **OK**.

9. Click on one of the group names, and in the **Active Field** group select **Collapse Entire Field**, , to hide all individual data for towns and only show totals.

10. Double click **Wearside** to show the detail rows within the **Wearside** group.

11. Click on one of the group names and select **Expand Entire Field**, , to display all the individual data for towns.

 *Double clicking a group name, e.g. **Wearside**, toggles between **Collaspe** and **Expand** data for that group. Also the **+** and **-** to the left of the group name on the worksheet can be used to show or hide the detail.*

12. A **PivotTable** can be amended, the row, column or count data can be changed. To change the count data to replies from the town, on the **PivotTable Field List** under **Values** use the drop down to select **Remove Field** then drag **Reply** into the same **Values** area.

		F	M	Grand Total
3	**Count of Reply**			
4		F	M	Grand Total
5	⊟ **Other**			
6	Bristol		1	1
7	Carlisle		1	1
8	⊟ **Wearside**			
9	Durham	5	6	11
10	Sunderland	11	13	24
11	Washington	10	6	16
12	⊟ **Tyneside**			
13	Newcastle	4	7	11
14	South Shields	6	3	9
15	Tynemouth		2	2
16	**Grand Total**	36	39	75

*The **PivotTable** displays those who have replied by **Town** and by **Gender**.*

13. Close the workbook <u>without</u> saving.

Driving Lesson 59 - S.A.E.

This is not an ECDL test. Testing may only be carried out through certified ECDL test centres. This is a Self-Assessment Exercise. Try to complete it without any reference to the Driving Lessons in this section.

1. Open the workbook **Staff**.

2. Create a **PivotTable** in a new sheet, making sure that the **Table/Range** contains the cell range of the whole table.

3. Use **Department** as the row field and **Surname** as the values field to give a breakdown of manpower by department.

4. Insert a row into the original list (not at the end) and add your own details, assigning yourself to one of the existing departments.

5. Refresh the **PivotTable** to see the effect.

6. Print the **PivotTable**.

7. Amend the **PivotTable** by removing the **Count of Surname**, adding **Age** as the Column field and **Absence** as the new Values field.

8. Group the data into the following Age Groups; **Under 40**, **40 - 50**, and **Over 50**. Which age group is responsible for the most absences?

9. Print a copy of the amended **PivotTable**.

10. Close the workbook <u>without</u> saving.

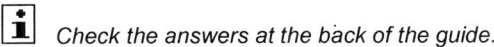 *Check the answers at the back of the guide.*

If you experienced any difficulty completing this S.A.E. refer back to the Driving Lessons in this section. Then redo the S.A.E.

Once you are confident with the features, complete the Record of Achievement Matrix referring to the section at the end of the guide. Only when competent move on to the next Section.

Section 13
Functions

By the end of this Section you should be able to:

Use Logical Functions

Use Date and Time Functions

Use Lookup Functions

Use Maths and Statistical Functions

Use Text Functions

Use Financial Functions

Use Database Functions

Use Nested Functions and Trends

To gain an understanding of the above features, work through the **Driving Lessons** in this **Section**.

For each **Driving Lesson**, read the **Park and Read** instructions, without touching the keyboard, then work through the numbered steps of the **Manoeuvres** on the computer. Complete the **S.A.E.** (Self-Assessment Exercise) at the end of the section to test your knowledge.

Driving Lesson 60 - Functions

🄿 Park and Read

Functions are specialised formulas that make calculations easier. They are grouped into categories, and some of the more common functions are listed here, grouped into the appropriate categories:

Statistical	COUNT, COUNTA, COUNTIF
Financial	NPV, FV, PMT, RATE, IRR
Logical	IF, OR, AND, TRUE, FALSE
Math & Trig	SUMIF, ROUND
Text	CONCATENATE, LOWER, PROPER, UPPER
Date & Time	TODAY, DAY, MONTH, YEAR, DATE, NOW, TIME
Database	DSUM, DMIN, DMAX, DCOUNT
Lookup & Reference	HLOOKUP, VLOOKUP

In general:

Statistical functions deal with analysing numerical data, from simple counting and averaging to calculating complex distribution parameters.

Financial functions deal mainly with calculations involving depreciation, loan repayments and investments over extended time scales.

Logical functions deal with the testing and setting of conditions involving **TRUE** or **FALSE** values.

Math & Trig functions deal with processing individual numerical data, from simple rounding to complex trigonometric calculations.

Text functions deal with manipulating text strings.

Date and Time functions deal with the processing and reformatting of all data relating to dates and times.

Database functions deal specifically with data, usually numeric, held in a list or database.

Lookup & Reference functions deal with mainly with data in tables or ranges, for example retrieving values or transposing vertical and horizontal ranges.

Functions, like formulas, are preceded by an = sign.

Functions can be used as values in calculations.

Functions can be used within other functions (nested functions).

Other spreadsheet applications may have different names for the same functions.

Driving Lesson 61 - Logical Functions

Park and Read

The logical function **IF** tests the contents of a cell and, if the logical test is met (TRUE condition), performs one action; if not (FALSE condition), it performs another.

=IF(Logical_test,Value_if_true,Value_if_false)

For instance, if the value in cell **A1** is greater than 10 then multiply it by 3, if not, multiply it by 2. This is expressed as: **=IF(A1>10,A1*3,A1*2)**

The **IF** function is sometimes described as **IF THEN ELSE**. **IF** the condition is true **THEN** do this **ELSE** do that.

AND and **OR** are logical functions that can be either **TRUE** or **FALSE**. **AND** tests 2 or more conditions and if <u>every</u> one is satisfied returns a value of **TRUE,** otherwise it returns a value of **FALSE**. So

=AND(A1>10,B1>10,C1>10)

is only **TRUE** if **A1** is greater than 10 <u>and</u> **B1** is greater than 10 <u>and</u> **C1** is greater than 10.

OR tests 2 or more conditions and if <u>any</u> one is satisfied returns a value of **TRUE,** otherwise it returns a value of **FALSE**. So

=OR(A1>10,B1>10,C1>10)

is **TRUE** if **A1** is greater than 10 <u>or</u> **B1** is greater than 10 <u>or</u> **C1** is greater than 10.

As the functions **AND** and **OR** return **TRUE** or **FALSE** values, they are often used in conjunction with **IF** functions in order to return a value for the logical test based on multiple conditions.

Manoeuvres

1. On a blank worksheet, enter the label **Interest Calculation** in **B1**.

2. Enter the label **Balance** in cell **B3** and **Interest** in **B4**.

3. Enter any number in **C3** for your bank balance.

4. The interest on your money depends on whether the balance is over or under **£100**. Click in cell **C4**.

5. Display the **Formulas** tab and in the **Function Library** group, click **Logical** and select **IF**.

i *The **Insert Function** button in the **Function Library** group and on the **Formula Bar** can be used to select a function using the **Insert Function** dialog box.*

Driving Lesson 61 - Continued

6.   Enter the following parts of the test with a mixture of pointing and typing into the **Function Arguments** dialog box.

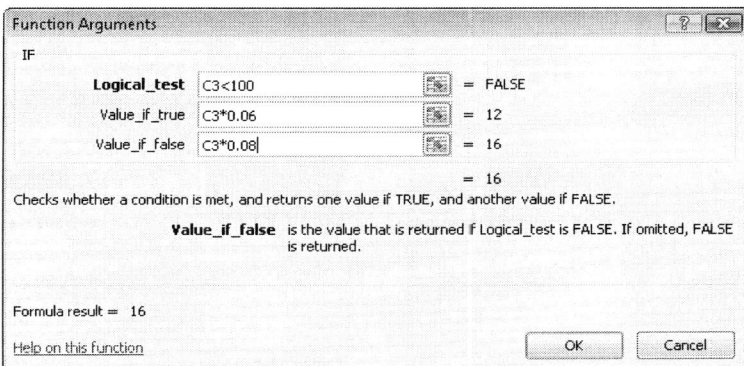

7.   Click **OK** to complete the function. The function looks at the contents of cell **C3** and if less than **100**, calculates the interest at **6%** otherwise it calculates it at **8%**.

8.   The result of the function, the interest, depends on the balance. Move to **C3** and enter **100**. The interest is **£8**, the higher rate. Enter **50** and the interest is **£3**. Experiment, change the balance and see the interest change.

9.   In cells **D5** to **D8**, enter a list of numbers **27**, **8**, **16**, **35**.

10.   In cell **F5** enter the logical function **=AND(D5>10,D5<20)** by keying or using **Insert Function**. This will return the value **TRUE** if both conditions (>10 and <20) are met and **FALSE** if they are not.

11.   Copy the function from **F5** to the range **F6** to **F8**. Only one cell value (**16**) meets both conditions.

12.   In cell **H5** enter the logical function **=OR(D5<10,D5>20)** by keying or using **Insert Function**. This will return the value **TRUE** if either condition (<10 or >20) is met and **FALSE** if not.

13.   Copy the function from **H5** to the range **H6** to **H8**. Only one cell value (**16**) does not meet either condition.

14.   Close the workbook <u>without</u> saving.

Driving Lesson 62 - Date and Time Functions

▣ Park and Read

Dates and times are stored as numbers of days since 00:00 on 1st Jan 1900. Calculations using dates and times are carried out using the numbers which represent the dates and times. There are two key presses which automatically insert the current date and time.

<Ctrl ;>	Inserts the current date as text.
<Ctrl Shift ;>	Inserts the current time as text.

There are also several functions for use purely with dates and times.

DATE	Returns the number for a particular day, e.g. DATE(92,4,13) returns 33707, the number of days from 1st Jan 1900 to 13th Apr. 1992.
DAY, MONTH,YEAR	Converts a date to a number representing the day, month, or year, e.g. DAY("23/11/67") would be 23.
NOW	Used as NOW(). Returns the current date and time as a number, and is updated as the worksheet is calculated.
DATEVALUE	Converts the date as text to a number, e.g. DATEVALUE("21-Sept-49") returns 18162.
TODAY	Used as TODAY(). Returns the current date as a number and is updated as the worksheet is calculated.
WEEKDAY	Converts a number to an integer representing the day of the week from 1 (Sunday) to 7 (Saturday), e.g. WEEKDAY("21-Sept-49") returns 4, Wednesday.
TIME	Used as TIME(hour,minute,second). Returns a value in the range 0 to 0.99999999, representing a fraction of a day, e.g. TIME(16,48,10) returns 0.700115741.
TIMEVALUE	Returns a number as a fraction of the day, e.g.TIMEVALUE("22nd-Aug-67 6:35 am") returns .274305556.
HOUR, MINUTE,SECOND	Converts a time into hours, minutes, or seconds, e.g. HOUR("6:35pm") returns 18.

Driving Lesson 62 - Continued

⌐▷ Manoeuvres

1. Open a new workbook. This Driving Lesson shows some of the described functions in action.

2. In **B2**, enter the label **Time as number**. In **D2**, enter **Time as text**.

3. In **B4**, enter **=NOW()** and format it to display as **hh:mm:ss**. In the **Home** tab, **Number** group, and from the General drop down select **Time**.

4. In **D4**, press <**Ctrl Shift ;**> to enter the current time.

5. In **B8**, enter the function **=TIME(8,30,0)** and custom format to display as **hh:mm**.

6. In **B12**, enter **=B4-B8** to calculate an elapsed time. Format the value as **Time**.

7. The **Time as number** and **Time as text** should now appear as different times. This is because the function **NOW()** is updated as the worksheet is calculated, while using <**Ctrl Shift ;**> puts text in the sheet, which is not updated.

8. In **F2**, enter **=TODAY()**.

9. In **F4**, enter **=DATE(** then your date of birth as numbers in the form **yy,mm,dd** followed by a **)**.

10. In **F8**, enter **=F2-F4**. Format the cell as a number with no decimal places. This shows your age in days.

11. In **H4**, enter **=WEEKDAY(F4)**. This gives a number corresponding to the day of the week on which you were born (Sunday = 1, Saturday = 7). Add a **Custom** format to cell **H4** of **dddd**.

12. In **J4** enter **=DAY(F4)** to extract the day part of your birth date.

13. In **J5** enter **=MONTH(F4)** to extract the month part of your birth date.

14. In **J6** enter **=YEAR(F4)** to extract the year part of your birth date.

15. Close the workbook <u>without</u> saving.

Driving Lesson 63 - Lookup Functions

 Park and Read

The **Lookup** functions are used to look up relevant data from a table, to use in a calculation. There are two functions, **HLOOKUP**, which searches a horizontal table and **VLOOKUP**, which searches a vertical table.

A **Lookup** table consists of a selection of bands, or intervals, within which a given value can be found.

Manoeuvres

1. Open the workbook **Discount**. The worksheet consists of a discount calculation at the top and two lookup tables at the bottom, one a horizontal and one a vertical, containing the same data. The discount to be used (in **D8**) depends directly on the number of items bought.

2. To look up the discount from the horizontal table using the **HLOOKUP** function, click in cell **D8**.

3. Click the **Lookup & Reference** button and select the function **HLOOKUP**.

4. The **Lookup_value** is cell **D4** (number bought). The **Table_array** is **C14:I15** (the table without the labels) and the **Row_index_num** is **2** (to return the value from the 2nd row of the table).

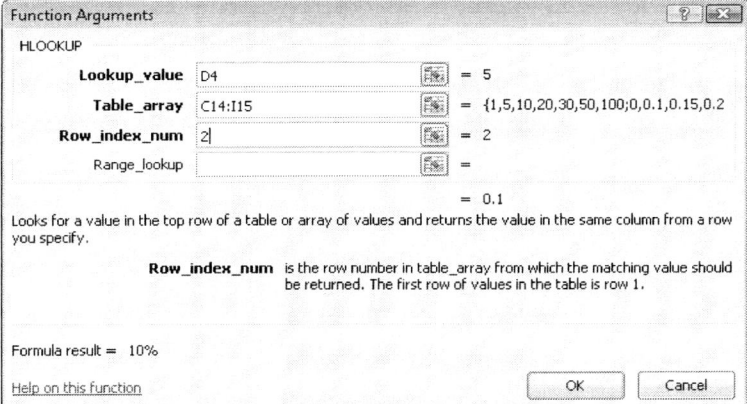

 *Setting the **Range_lookup** to **FALSE** causes the function to return a value only if there is an <u>exact</u> match between the **Lookup_value** and the table entry.*

5. Click **OK**.

Driving Lesson 63 - Continued

6. The value returned is **10**%, corresponding to selling between 5 and 9 items.

7. Change the number bought in **D4** to **23**. The **Discount %** changes, and so does the **Discount Price**.

8. Delete the contents of cell **D8**.

9. To use the **VLOOKUP** function on the vertical table, click in cell **D8**.

10. Click the **Lookup & Reference** button and select the function **VLOOKUP** (this function is similar to **HLOOKUP** except the base data is stored in columns).

11. The **Lookup_value** is cell **D4** (number bought). The **Table_array** is **B19:C25** (the table without the labels) and the **Col_index_num** is **2** (to return the value from the 2nd column of the table).

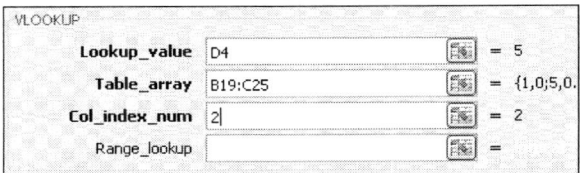

12. Click **OK** to complete the function.

13. Change the number bought in **D4** to **52**. The **Discount %** changes to **45%** the **Discount Price** is **£2000.57**.

14. Close the workbook <u>without</u> saving.

Driving Lesson 64 - Maths and Statistical Functions

 Park and Read

The **Count** function counts the numeric items in a range of cells. **Counta** is used to count all cells in a range. **Countif** counts numeric items that match a set condition.

Sumif only sums values within a range that match a set condition, e.g. to sum the outstanding amounts for clients that owe more than £100. **Round** can be used to round a numeric value to any number of figures.

Manoeuvres

1. Open the workbook **Invoices**.

2. Select cell **A16**.

3. Click the **More Functions** button, select **Statistical** and then select the function **COUNT** to display the **Function Arguments** box for **COUNT**.

4. Select the **Value1** as **A6:A14**.

5. Click **OK** to display the count of invoices, (9). This works because column **A** contains numeric values.

6. Copy the function in **A16** to **D16**. The count will be zero because column **D** is not numeric.

7. Select **D16** and edit the contents, changing **COUNT** to **COUNTA**. The total should now be correctly shown as 9.

8. Delete the contents of cell **D16** and enter the label **Invoices under £500**.

9. Select cell **E16**.

10. Click the **More Functions** button, select **Statistical** and then select the function **COUNTIF** to display the **Function Arguments** box for **COUNTIF**.

11. Select the **Range** as **E6:E14**.

12. Set the criteria in the **Criteria** box as **<500**.

Driving Lesson 64 - Continued

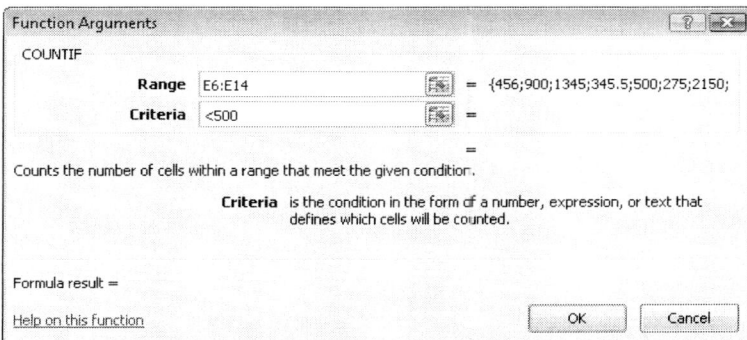

13. Click **OK**. Check the **Formula Bar** for the formula (the speech marks are added automatically). The cells that match the condition are counted. The result is **4**. These cells can also be summed using **SUMIF**.

14. In cell **D17**, enter the label **Small invoices total**.

15. Select cell **E17**.

16. Click the **Math & Trig** button and select the function **SUMIF** to display the **Function Arguments** box for **SUMIF**.

17. Select the **Range** as **E6:E14**.

18. In the **Criteria** box enter **<500**.

19. Click **OK** to insert the function. The invoices that are under £500 are summed. The formula is similar to **COUNTIF** except that the cells are added. The sum of the four invoices is **1454.50**.

20. To show the invoice totals to the nearest pound, select cell **H6**. Click the **Math & Trig** button and select the function **ROUND** to display the **Function Arguments** box for **ROUND**.

21. Select the **Number** as **G6**.

22. Set the number of digits in the **Num_digits** box as **0**.

23. Click **OK** to insert the function. The invoice total is shown to the nearest pound.

24. Copy the function in **H6** to fill the range **H7** to **H14**.

⚟ *Even though the values in column **H** have been rounded to the nearest pound, they are still displayed in the original number format.*

25. Close the workbook <u>without</u> saving.

Driving Lesson 65 - Text Functions

Park and Read

The ampersand symbol, **&**, or the **CONCATENATE** function can be used to bring together the contents of two or more cells that contain text. Other text manipulation functions are used to change text entries into the required form. **LOWER(string)** changes the entry into lower case. **UPPER(string)** changes the entry into upper case (capitals) and **PROPER(string)** changes the entry into lower case with capital first letters.

These functions are used when data is required in a different format to that which has been entered or imported.

Manoeuvres

1.   Open the workbook **Strings**.

2.   In **B10**, enter the formula **=B4&C4&D4**. The words in these cells are joined together, but with no spaces.

3.   In **B11**, enter the function **=B4&" "&C4&" "&D4**. Each set of speech marks is around one space. This adds the spaces between the text.

4.   The function **CONCATENATE** can be used to achieve the same result. In **B12**, enter the formula **=CONCATENATE(B4," ",C4," ",D4)** to achieve exactly the same effect as step 3.

5.   The **Ref No**. is to be made up of the initials of the customer added to the invoice number. In **H4** enter the function **=LEFT(C4,1)&LEFT(D4,1)&E4**. This gives an individual reference number.

6.   Copy the formula in **H4** down to **H5** and **H6**.

7.   Click on the **Text** worksheet and in cell **B2**, type (in lower case) **upper**, in **C2** type **lower** and in **D2** type **proper**.

8.   In **B4** enter the function **=UPPER(B2)**. The word "UPPER" will appear in capitals, i.e. upper case.

9.   In **C4** enter the function **=LOWER(C2)**. The word "lower" stays the same, in lower case.

10. In **D4** enter the function **=PROPER(D2)**. This produces the word "**Proper**" with a capital **P**.

11. Enter a phrase (a few words) into the cell **B2**, copy the cell to the range **C2:D2**. Examine the results in cells **B4, C4** and **D4**.

12. Change the text in cell **B2** to see different text displayed in **Upper, Lower** and **Proper** case.

13. Close the workbook <u>without</u> saving.

Driving Lesson 66 - Financial Functions

▣ Park and Read

Three of the many financial functions deal with the repayment of loans. If **pv** is the present (original) value of the loan, **rate** is the interest rate per period, **nper** is the total number of payments and **pmt** is the repayment per period, the following functions can be used.

=PMT(rate,nper,pv).	Calculates repayments if **rate**, **nper** and **pv** are known.
=RATE(nper,pmt,pv).	Calculates the rate if **pmt**, **nper** and **pv** are known.
=PV(rate,nper,pmt,).	Calculates the loan value if **rate**, **pmt** and **nper** are known.

Similar functions deal with the results of investing or saving:

=FV(rate,nper,pmt)	Calculates the final value of saving an amount **pmt** for **nper** periods at **rate** percent interest.
=NPV(rate,value1,value2,..)	Calculates the net present value of an investment using a comparison d scount rate of **rate** and a series of future income payments (positive values) and payments (negative values).

⌢ Manoeuvres

1. Open a new workbook in which a loan repayment is to be calculated.

2. In **C2** enter the label **LOAN ANALYSIS**.

3. In **C4** enter **Interest Rate**.

4. In **C6** enter **Term (months)**.

5. In **C8** enter **Loan Amount**.

6. In **E4** enter the interest rate as **6%**.

7. The **Term** is the length of the loan. Enter **360** into **E6** (30 years).

8. In **E8** enter the size of the loan, **£50000**.

9. In **C10**, enter the label **Monthly Repayment**.

10. In **C11**, click the **Financial** button and select the function **PMT**.

Driving Lesson 66 - Continued

11. Complete the dialog box as below:

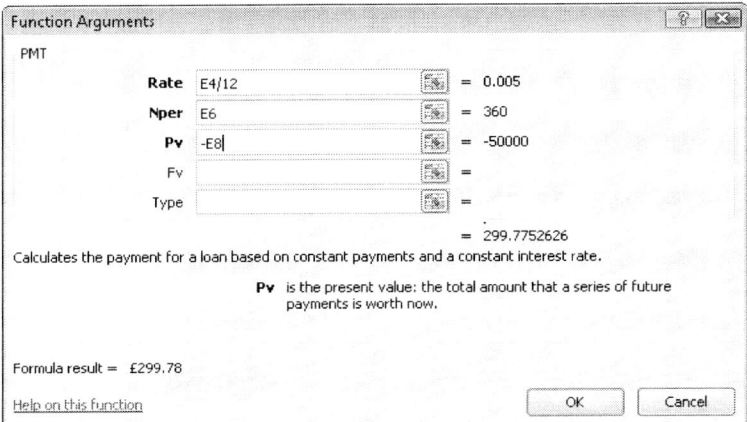

12. The **Rate** is divided by 12 to obtain a monthly rate, and the **Amount** is entered as negative because the loan is an amount owed. Click **OK** to complete the function.

13. Change the interest rate to **8%**.

14. If the maximum affordable repayment is **£300**, the maximum loan value can be calculated using **PV**.

15. In **G4** enter **8%**, in **G6** enter **360** and in **G10** enter **300**.

16. In **G8** enter the function **=PV(G4/12,G6,-G10)** to see the maximum amount that can be borrowed.

17. To see the result of investing the same amount of money under the same conditions, in **I8** enter the function **=FV(G4/12,G6,-G10)**.

18. Save this workbook as **Loan Analysis**.

19. Close the workbook.

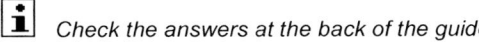 *Check the answers at the back of the guide.*

Driving Lesson 67 - Database Functions

🄿 Park and Read

There are functions especially designed to be used with lists. The functions perform calculations on fields in a list, but <u>only</u> on those records which meet the selection conditions defined in the criteria range. For example in a list of sales by city, database functions can be used to obtain values for a specific city only, by selecting that city in the criteria range. The available functions are as follows:

Function	Results
DAVERAGE	Averages numbers
DCOUNT	Counts numbers
DCOUNTA	Counts nonblank cells
DGET	Extracts a single value
DMAX	Finds a maximum value
DMIN	Finds a minimum value
DPRODUCT	Multiplies numbers
DSTDEV	Calculates standard deviation of a sample
DSUM	Adds numbers
DVAR	Calculates variance of a sample

🄿 Manoeuvres

1. Open the workbook **Survey**.

2. To find information about people who have replied to the survey, copy the top line of the list, the titles, to row **2**. Rows **2** and **3** will be the area (criteria range) where the selection criteria for the functions will be set.

3. Enter **1** in **G3**, under **Reply** (only include records where **Reply** = '**1**').

4. In **I2** enter the label **Replies**, in **I4**, **Oldest**, in **I6**, **Youngest**, in **I8**, **Total** and in **I10**, **Average**.

5. Select the cell **J2** and click **Insert Function** button.

6. The **Insert Function** dialog box is displayed. Choose the category **Database** and the function **DCOUNT** from the list. Click **OK**. The **DCOUNT** dialog box is then displayed.

Driving Lesson 67 - Continued

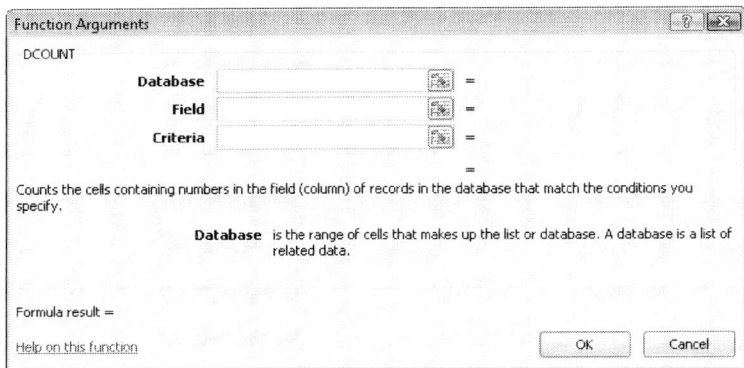

7. In **Database** enter **A5:G225,** in **field** click on **G5**.

8. In the **criteria** box, point or enter **A2:G3**.

9. Click **OK** to display the total number of replies.

10. Follow the same procedure to find the oldest person to reply. In **J4** enter = **DMAX(A5:G225,E5,A2:G3)**. Check the age field to confirm the answer.

11. In **J6** enter **=DMIN(A5:G225,E5,A2:G3)**. This displays the age of the youngest person to reply. Check the age field to confirm the answer.

12. In **J8** enter **=DSUM(A5:G225,E5,A2:G3)**. This displays the total age of all persons who have replied.

13. In **J10** enter **=DAVERAGE(A5:G225,E5,A2:G3)**. This displays the average age of all persons who have replied.

14. Close the workbook without saving.

i *Some of the answers in this Driving Lesson are rather vague as the worksheet contains the **Now** function to calculate ages from dates of birth. Everyone is getting older by the day, therefore the sum of their ages and the average age are increasing day by day.*

i *Check the answers at the back of the guide.*

Driving Lesson 68 - Nested Functions

 Park and Read

Individual functions can be combined with each other to form more complex functions. When one of the values within a function is itself a function, this is known as a **Nested Function**. An example of nested text functions is **=UPPER(LEFT(B2,3)**, which would return the upper case of the left three characters in the cell **B2**.

A common use for nested functions is in the **IF** function, where the logical test, e.g. **A1>10** can be replaced by a logical function, e.g. **AND(A1>10,A1<20)**.

It is vital that the nested function returns a value of the same type as required by the first function or an error will result. In the first example, **LEFT** returns a text field, which is required for the **UPPER** function; and in the second example, **AND** returns a logical value (TRUE or FALSE) which is required as the first value for the **IF** function.

Manoeuvres

1. Open the workbook **Employees**.

2. It is decided to pay a £15 bonus to all employees 40 or over who have had less than 2 days absence this year.

3. Enter the label **Bonus** in cell **G1**.

4. Select cell **G2** and click the **Logical** button and select the function **IF** to display the **IF** box.

5. In the **Logical_test** field enter the function **AND(E2>=40,F2<2)**.

6. Enter **15** in the **Value_if_true** field and **0** in the **Value_if_false**.

7. Click **OK** to enter the function.

8. Copy the nested functions from **G2** to the range **G3** to **G20** to see who qualifies for the bonus.

9. Close the workbook <u>without</u> saving.

 Check the answers at the back of the guide.

Driving Lesson 69 - Trends

Park and Read

One useful analysis tool which can be applied to spreadsheet data is the ability to calculate trends. For a series of (usually) time based data values, it is possible to mathematically calculate the underlying trend of the data. The main purpose of this is usually to extend the trend and predict future values.

It is possible to calculate trends on the data directly or graphically on a chart.

Manoeuvres

1. Open the workbook **Trend**. This shows some sales figures for the first five months of the year. You need to calculate the trend of the data over the five months and predict the trend in sales for the next three months.

2. Highlight the range **B5:I5**.

3. Click the **More Functions** button, select **Statistical** then select the function **Trend**.

4. Fill in the required parameters. The **Known_y's** are the available actual values, **B4:F4**. The **Known_x's** are the available time periods, **B3:F3**. The **New_x's** are the time periods for the calculated trend, **B3:I3**. Leave **Const** blank.

5. **Trend** is an array function. It applies to a selected range of values, not just a single cell. To enter the function into the range, hold down <**Ctrl**> and <**Shift**> and press <**Enter**>.

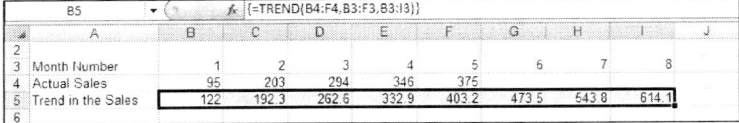

	A	B	C	D	E	F	G	H	I	J
2										
3	Month Number	1	2	3	4	5	6	7	8	
4	Actual Sales	95	203	294	346	375				
5	Trend in the Sales	122	192.3	262.6	332.9	403.2	473.5	543.8	614.1	
6										

B5 = {=TREND(B4:F4,B3:F3,B3:I3)}

Excel places brackets { } around the formula to show it is an array formula.

Alternatively type in the formula =TREND(B4:F4,B3:F3,B3:I3) and hold down <Ctrl> and <Shift> then press and release <Enter>.

The trend calculation assumes a linear (straight line) relationship for the data.

6. The same analysis can be done on graphical data.

7. The chart on the **Trend** spreadsheet shows the actual data from the table above as a 2D column chart. Click on the chart and on the **Layout** tab, in the **Analysis** group, click **Trendline**.

Driving Lesson 69 - Continued

8.   There is a choice of types of trends that can be applied to the chart data. Select **Linear Trendline**.

9.   Select **Trendline** then **More Trendline Options**.

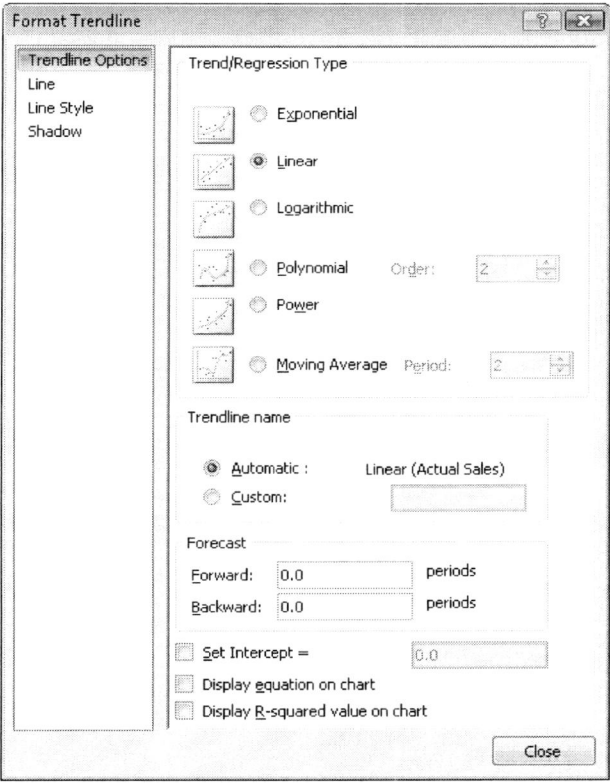

10.   Set the **Forecast Forward** to **3** periods and select the **Display R-squared value** option. R-squared is a measure of how well the calculated trend fits with the actual data. 1 = a perfect fit.

11.   Click **Close** to draw the trendline. R-squared is shown as **0.946** which is quite a good fit, but maybe a different prediction would be even better.

12.   Click away from the first trendline and select **Trendline** then **More Trendline Options** again but this time select the **Logarithmic** type.

Driving Lesson 69 - Continued

13. Set the **Forward Forecast** to **3** periods and select the **Display R-squared value** option. Click **Close**. A second trendline is drawn and this time the fit is much better, **0.994**.

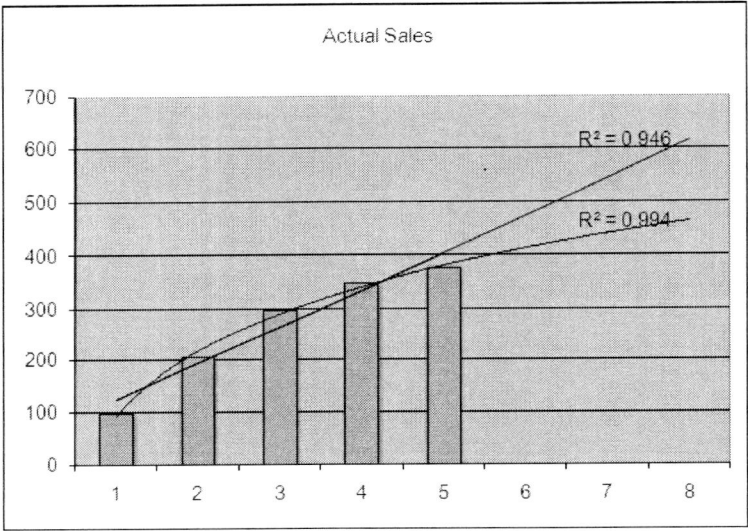

14. This chart shows the dangers of mathematical prediction. Depending on which trendline is used, the predicted figures for month 8 sales can be quite different.

15. Close the workbook <u>without</u> saving.

Driving Lesson 70 - S.A.E.

This is not an ECDL test. Testing may only be carried out through certified ECDL test centres. This is a Self-Assessment Exercise. Try to complete it without any reference to the Driving Lessons in this section.

1. Open the workbook **Employees**, insert two rows at the top of the sheet and copy the column headers to the new **Row 1**.

2. In **F24** use the **COUNTIF** function to calculate the number of staff over 40 years. Manually check the age column to confirm the answer.

3. In **F25** calculate the same value using the **DCOUNT** function. Use **rows 1** and **2** as the **Criteria** range.

4. In **F26** use the **DAVERAGE** function to find the average age of staff over 40.

5. In **F27** use the **ROUND** function to display the average age from **F26** to the nearest whole number.

6. Without altering the functions, find the **DCOUNT** and **DAVERAGE** values for staff over 30.

7. Create the lookup table and use **HLOOKUP** to calculate an attendance bonus (**Bonus 1**) in **Column G** based on; 0-2 days absence, £50; 3-5 days, £25, 6 or more days, £0.

Absence	0	3	6
Bonus	£50	£25	£0

   (When copying a **HLOOKUP** function down a column, remember to use absolute addressing for the lookup table.)

8. In **Column H** calculate a stress bonus (**Bonus 2**) which is **£100** for all staff in Finance or Training and **£20** for everyone else, using the **IF** function with a nested **OR** function.
   Example answer =IF(OR(D4="Finance",D4="Training"),100,20).

9. Format **Column I** as numeric with 0 decimal places. In this column use the **YEAR** function to find the year of birth for each staff member and add 60 to it. Name the column **Retirement Year**.

10. In **Column J** use the **CONCATENATE** function to join together **First** name and **Surname** with a space between them. Widen the cells to fit the largest name and name the column **Full Name**.

11. Save the workbook as **Employees2** and then close it.

If you experienced any difficulty completing this S.A.E. refer back to the Driving Lessons in this section. Then redo the S.A.E.

Once you are confident with the features, complete the Record of Achievement Matrix referring to the section at the end of the guide. Only when competent move on to the next Section.

Section 14
Charts

By the end of this Section you should be able to:

Format Charts

Modify Charts

Insert Images in 2D Charts

To gain an understanding of the above features, work through the **Driving Lessons** in this **Section**.

For each **Driving Lesson**, read the **Park and Read** instructions, without touching the keyboard, then work through the numbered steps of the **Manoeuvres** on the computer. Complete the **S.A.E.** (Self-Assessment Exercise) at the end of the section to test your knowledge.

Driving Lesson 71 - Formatting Charts

Park and Read

All parts of a chart, including the colours, axes, text, gridlines, background, etc., can be changed.

Manoeuvres

1. Open the workbook **Charts**.

2. Click on the **Sales Chart** sheet tab to display the chart that has been created on a new sheet, then click anywhere on the chart to select it.

3. Move the cursor under the lower axis of the chart, until the **ToolTip** reads **Horizontal (Category) Axis**. Click to select the horizontal axis. On the **Format** tab, in the **Current Selection** group, click **Format Selection** to display the **Format Axis** dialog box.

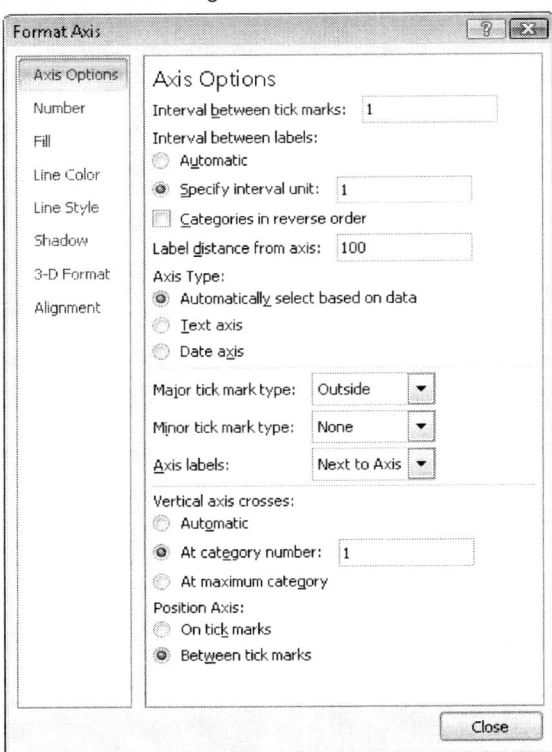

Driving Lesson 71 - Continued

4. In **Axis Options**, select the **Major tick mark type** as a **Cross** and the **Minor tick mark type** as **Inside**. From **Line Color**, select a dark blue **Color**. In **Line Style**, select the width as **2pt**. Click **Close** to see the effects.

5. With the horizontal axis still selected, right click to display the shortcut menus. Select **Italic** style, **Red** colour and size **12**. The changes are shown as they are made. Click away from the selection to close the menu.

6. Click on one of the columns on the chart. Make sure all columns are selected. If not, click away then retry. On the **F̲ormat** tab, in the **Current Selection** group, click **Format Selection** to display the **Format Data Series** dialog box.

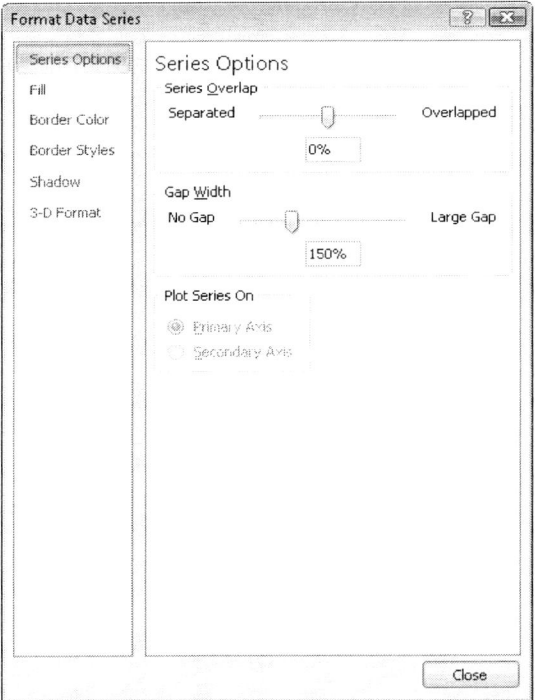

7. From the **Fill** section, a variety of borders, colours and fill effects can be applied to the data columns. Change the colour to pale green and close the dialog box.

8. With the data series still selected right click to display the shortcut menu. Select **Add Data Labels**. The data labels are added to the columns.

Driving Lesson 71 - Continued

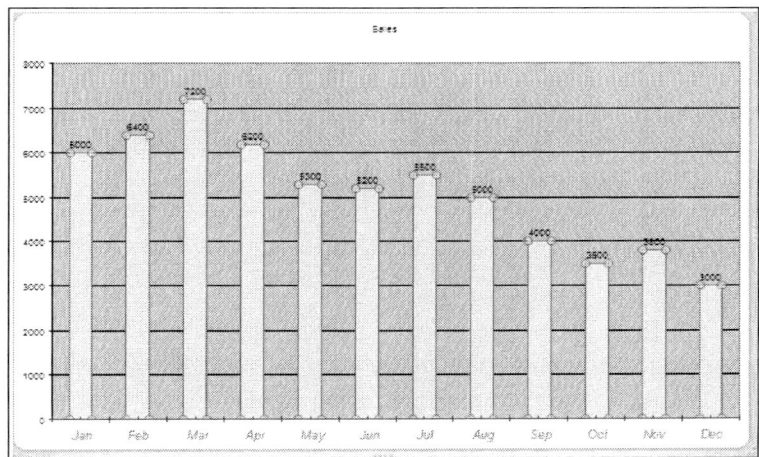

9. **Data labels** are now shown and can be formatted like any other chart component. Click any **Data label** to select them all, right click and select **Format Data Labels** from the shortcut menu.

10. In the **Label Options** section, from the **Label Position** area, select **Inside End** and click **Close**.

11. The chart title is **Sales** at the top centre. Right click on the title and change the **Font** to **blue, bold** and the font size to **20**.

12. Right click on the title and select **Format Chart Title**. Select **Solid fill** and choose a **pale yellow** background from the **Color** drop down. Click **Close**.

13. To reposition the chart title, click on the edge of the title, the cursor changes to a four pointed arrow and drag slightly to the left.

14. To add a **Legend** to the chart, on the **Layout** tab, **Labels** group, click the **Legend** button. Select **Show Legend at Right**. The legend is displayed on the chart.

15. Reposition the legend further up, away from the columns, using the same method used to move the chart title.

16. Leave the workbook open for the next lesson.

Driving Lesson 72 - Modifying Charts

 ## Park and Read

As well as formatting the components of a chart, the chart type may be modified either globally or for individual data series. Individual data series may be removed from a chart, although this does not affect the original source data.

 ## Manoeuvres

1. The workbook **Charts** should still be open. If not open it.

2. Make the **TvS Chart** active. Select the chart, without selecting a data series. On the **Design** tab, in the **Type** group, click **Change Chart Type**.

3. The current option is displayed, i.e. **3-D Clustered Column**. Select the first option, **Clustered Column** to change the chart type from 3D to 2D. Click **OK**.

4. Click the **'Turnover'** data series (blue), making sure all columns are selected and redisplay the **Chart Type** options.

5. Select the chart style **Line with Markers**. Click **OK**. Now one data series is shown as columns and one as a line chart.

6. Very carefully position the cursor on the line of the **'Turnover'** data series.

7. Right click to display a shortcut menu and select **Delete** from the resulting menu to remove the series from the chart.

*Alternatively, on the **Design** tab, **Data** group, click **Select Data**. Select the series to delete, and click the **Remove** button. Click **OK** to close the dialog box.*

8. Change the **Chart Type** for the remaining series to a basic **Pie Chart**.

9. Select one of the multi-coloured **Chart Styles** from the **Design** tab so that the chart segments can be seen.

10. Click and drag any segment out from the centre. The whole pie chart will be exploded.

11. Click away from the chart segments then push any segment back to reform the chart.

12. Click again on a single segment to select it. One segment can now be dragged out and pushed back.

13. Right click on a segment and select **Format Data Series**.

14. With **Series Options** selected, drag the slider for **Angle of first slice** to about 90^0. The angle of the slices is changed. Click **Close**.

15. Save the workbook as **Charts2** and close it.

Driving Lesson 73 - Insert Image in 2D Chart

▣ Park and Read

The use of images can greatly enhance the impact of charts. They can be used with any component of the chart but in practice they are most commonly used as backgrounds (the **Plot Area**) or as data columns (**Data Series**).

⌒ Manoeuvres

1.   Open the workbook **Charts** again and make the **Sales Chart** active.

2.   Click to select <u>all</u> data columns (**Series "Sales"**) and right click and select **Format Data Series**.

3.   In the **Series Options** section reduce the **Gap width** to approximately 100% by dragging the **Gap Width** slider slightly to the left.

4.   In the **Fill** section, select the **Picture or texture fill** option and then click the **File** button under **Insert from**.

5.   Find the image **Sales.gif** within the data files folder and double click or click and **Insert** to retrieve it. One image fills each column. Click **Close**.

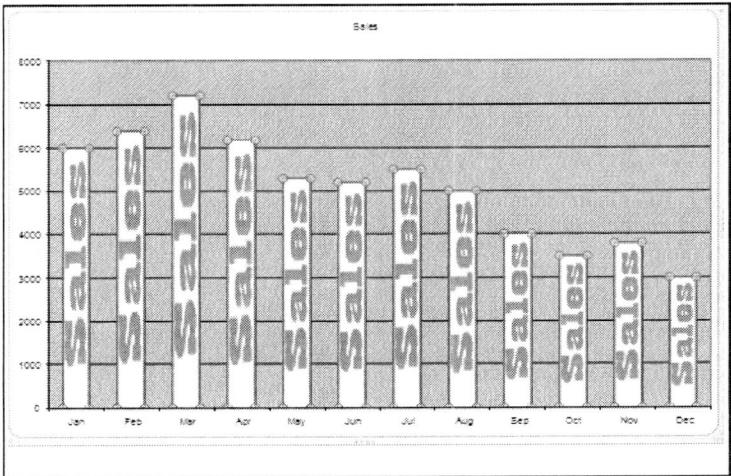

6.   To see the effect of an image as background, select the **Plot Area** of the chart right click and select **Format Plot Area**.

7.   In the **Fill** section repeat the process to insert the graphic file **Cialogo.jpg** on the plot area. Click **Close**.

8.   Close the workbook <u>without</u> saving.

Driving Lesson 74 - S.A.E.

This is not an ECDL test. Testing may only be carried out through certified ECDL test centres. This is a Self-Assessment Exercise. Try to complete it without any reference to the Driving Lessons in this section.

1.　Open workbook **Hotel**.

2.　Select the range **A4:M6** and use the **Charts** group dialog box launcher from the **Insert** tab to display the **Insert Chart** dialog box. Produce a 2D column chart for the selected data series.

3.　Add a chart a title '**Room Bookings**' and move the chart to a new sheet, using the **Move Chart** button on the **Design** tab.

4.　Click and drag the chart title into a space in the upper left of the chart area. Click and drag the legend to the upper right.

5.　Select the **Vertical (Value) Axis**. Change the line to be a thick red line and change the font to be red italic.

6.　Select the **Plot Area** and apply a light coloured textured background.

7.　Select one set of data columns and change the gap width to approximately **70%**. This should widen both data series columns.

8.　Select the **Double Room** data series and change the chart type to a line chart for that series only.

9.　Right click the line chart and remove it.

10.　Select the remaining data series and add **Data labels**. Format the labels to include the **Category Name**.

11.　Remove the **Legend**.

12.　Set the page orientation to **Landscape** if not already set, check the print preview and then print a copy of the chart.

13.　Change the chart type to a **Pie in 2-D** chart.

14.　Select only the segment for **August** and drag it out from the rest to explode it.

15.　Close down the workbook <u>without</u> saving.

If you experienced any difficulty completing this S.A.E. refer back to the Driving Lessons in this section. Then redo the S.A.E.

Once you are confident with the features, complete the Record of Achievement Matrix referring to the section at the end of the guide. Only when competent move on to the next Section.

Section 15
Data Tables

By the end of this Section you should be able to:

Create a One Input Data Table

Create a Two Input Data Table

To gain an understanding of the above features, work through the **Driving Lessons** in this **Section**.

For each **Driving Lesson**, read the **Park and Read** instructions, without touching the keyboard, then work through the numbered steps of the **Manoeuvres** on the computer. Complete the **S.A.E.** (Self-Assessment Exercise) at the end of the section to test your knowledge.

Driving Lesson 75 - One Input Data Table

Park and Read

A **Data Table** is used to see how changing one variable in a formula affects the result of that formula, e.g. "How do the repayments on a loan change for different interest rates?" By using a **Data Table**, the calculation need only be done once and the results of numerous different rates can be seen.

 Any function can be used as the starting point for a data table.

Manoeuvres

1. Open the workbook **Loan**. The calculation in **C11** shows the repayment amount for a loan, based on the values in **E4**, **E6** and **E8**. This Driving Lesson creates a **Data Table** showing how the result varies for a range of one of these values (**E4**, interest rate).

2. In **B12** enter an interest rate of **4%**.

3. Highlight the range **B12:B36** and on the **Home** tab, **Editing** group, click **Fill** and then **Series**. Enter a **Step value** of **0.0025**. Click **OK** and this enters a list of interest rates rising in ¼ percentage points.

4. Format the range **B12:B36** as percentages to **2** decimal places.

5. Highlight the range **B11:C36** (the range of the **Data Table** includes the calculated cell) and on the **Data** tab, **Data Tools** group, click **What-If Analysis** and then **Data Table**.

6. The values to be substituted are in a column, click in the **Column input cell** box. The value in the calculation which is actually changing down the column, is the interest rate, so click on cell **E4** to select it.

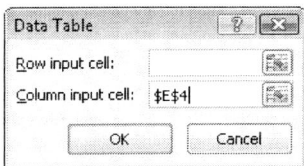

7. Click **OK**.

8. The table of values is automatically filled in, calculating the repayments for each of the different interest rates. Format the repayment figures, in column **C**, as **currency** (2 decimal places). Change the **Loan Amount** to **£60000**. The whole table is automatically recalculated.

9. Save the workbook as **Loan2** and leave it open for the next lesson.

Driving Lesson 76 - Two Input Data Table

▣ Park and Read

A two-input data table is used to see how the results of a formula change as two of the input values are varied. For instance, as well as varying the interest rate of a loan, what affect does the length of the loan have on repayments? A two input data table needs inputs for both the row and column of the table.

⌐ Manoeuvres

1. The workbook **Loan2** should still be open, if not, open it. Change the **Loan Amount** back to **£50,000**.

2. Select and delete the existing results range **C12:C36**.

> **i** *Part of a **Data Table** cannot be deleted. To delete a **Data Table**, the whole range must be selected.*

3. Cut and paste the cell **C11** to **B11**.

4. In **C11** enter **120,** this is 10 years expressed in months. Use **Fill Series** on the range **C11:G11**, with a step value of **60** (5 year intervals) to fill in the top row of the table.

5. Highlight the range **B11:G36** and on the **Data** tab, **Data Tools** group, click **What-If Analysis** and then **Data Table**.

6. In this table there are two variable inputs: a row and a column. In **Row Input Cell**, enter **E6** (the loan term). The **Column Input Cell** is **E4** (the interest rate, as before). Click on **OK**. The table is instantly completed.

7. Format the table appropriately. It is now possible to see at a glance how changes in interest rates **and** loan terms alter repayments. For example the monthly repayment on £50,000 over 20 years at 5.00% is **£329.99**.

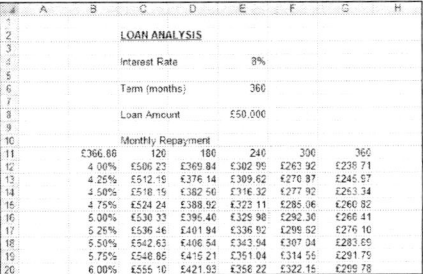

8. Save the workbook using the same filename (**Loan2**) and close it.

> **i** *This example uses the **PMT** (payment) function in the **Data Table**, but any function can be used as the basis for an input data table.*

Driving Lesson 77 - S.A.E.

This is not an ECDL test. Testing may only be carried out through certified ECDL test centres. This is a Self-Assessment Exercise. Try to complete it without any reference to the Driving Lessons in this section.

1. Open a new workbook.

2. In **C1** enter **No. Rooms** , in **C2** enter **Charged** and in **C3** enter **Overhead**.

3. In **E5** enter **Price Charged** and in **A12** enter **Occupied**.

4. In **B8** enter **1** and using **Series**, produce the numbers **1** to **10** in the range **B8:B17**. This represents the number of rooms occupied.

5. In **C7:H7** enter the numbers **15** to **20** to represent the possible charges made for each room.

6. This table will calculate the profitability of the hotel, depending on the fixed overheads, the room charge and how many rooms are occupied. In the top left of the table, the formula for calculating the profit must be entered. In **B7** enter **=D1*D2-D3**, in **D1** enter **1**, in **D2** enter **20** and in **D3** enter **100** (the actual values in **D1** and **D2** can be left blank).

7. Create the two-input data table.

8. Format the sheet appropriately. Format the data range **C8:H17** as currency, with negative numbers shown in red with a minus sign.

9. From the table, how many rooms in the Hotel must be occupied to guarantee a profit, regardless of the charge per room (within the charge range £15 to £20).

10. Change the overhead figure in **D3** to **130**.

11. At £20 per room the hotel is half full. Is it worth reducing the charges to £15 if this would mean it would be fully booked.

12. Obtain a printed copy.

13. Close the workbook <u>without</u> saving.

 Check the answers at the back of the guide.

If you experienced any difficulty completing this S.A.E. refer back to the Driving Lessons in this section. Then redo the S.A.E.

Once you are confident with the features, complete the Record of Achievement Matrix referring to the section at the end of the guide. Only when competent move on to the next Section.

Section 16
Macros

By the end of this Section you should be able to:

Understand Macros

Record a Macro

Run a Macro

Assign a Macro to the Quick Access Toolbar

To gain an understanding of the above features, work through the **Driving Lessons** in this **Section**.

For each **Driving Lesson**, read the **Park and Read** instructions, without touching the keyboard, then work through the numbered steps of the **Manoeuvres** on the computer. Complete the **S.A.E.** (Self-Assessment Exercise) at the end of the section to test your knowledge.

Driving Lesson 78 - Macros

Park and Read

A **Macro** is a sequence of commands which can be recorded and then played back when required. Macros are useful for automating routine tasks, simplifying complex worksheets, creating custom menus, dialog boxes and buttons and running other applications. **Macros** are usually created by recording the actual cell and menu selections themselves as they occur.

 *Once recorded, **Macros** are stored as instructions written in **Visual Basic** code. It is possible to amend **Macros**, or even create them directly, by editing this code.*

Excel has different macro security levels because of the potential threat from viruses. The default **Security Level** is set to **High**. This has to be reduced for this feature to work with the accompanying data files.

Manoeuvres

1. To check the level of **Macro Security**, the **Developer** tab has to be displayed. Click the **Office** button, then click the **Excel Options** button. In the **Popular** section check **Show Developer tab in the Ribbon**. Click **OK**.

2. On the **Developer** tab, in the **Code** group, click **Macro Security**.

3. Select **Enable all macros**. This security level will remain at this level until it is changed. Click **OK**.

 *You may wish to return the **Macro Security** to its original setting when you have completed this section.*

4. Open the workbook **Hockey**. This workbook already has macros attached to it.

5. The league table has just had some results added to it. To sort the league table, on the **Developer** tab, in the **Code** group, click **Macros** and choose **Sort_League**.

6. Click **Run** to carry out the sort. The league is sorted first by points, descending, then by goal difference and then by goals for.

7. Enter **Prepared by** and your full name in cell **A12**.

8. The command button **Print** on the worksheet has a **Print_League** macro attached. Click the **Print** button to print a copy of the league table.

9. Close the workbook **Hockey** without saving.

Driving Lesson 79 - Recording a Macro

 Park and Read

It is important when creating a macro, that it is planned out beforehand, as *Excel* records all cell and menu selections, including mistakes!

 Manoeuvres

1. Start a new workbook.

2. On the **Developer** tab, in the **Code** group, click **Record Macro** to display the **Record Macro** dialog box.

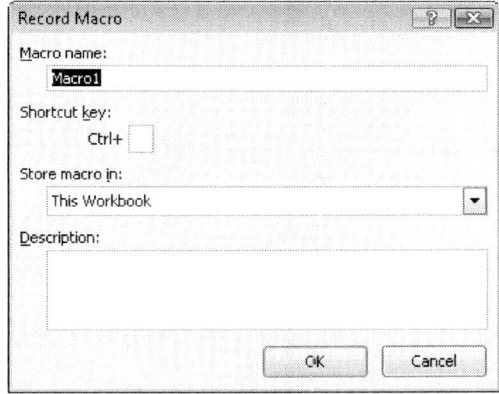

3. In the **Macro name** box, enter **Months**.

4. To assign a shortcut key, type **m** in the shortcut key box next to **Ctrl +**. This allows the macro to be run quickly with a **Ctrl+m** key press.

5. Leave the **Store macro in** box as **This Workbook** but drop down the list to see where macros can be stored.

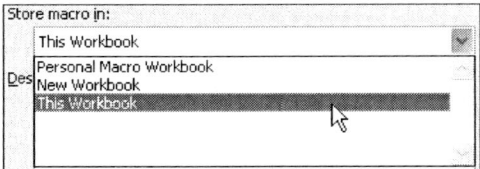

Driving Lesson 79 - Continued

i *This selection means that the macro is only available within this workbook. **New Workbook** is similar and macros will be restricted to that workbook. The **Personal Macro Workbook** is opened with **Excel** and the macros stored there are available to all open workbooks.*

6. Select **This Workbook** and click **OK**.

7. Every key press and mouse selection is now being recorded.

8. Press <**Ctrl Home**> to place the cursor in cell **A1** (even if it is there already). Use the right arrow key to move to cell **B1** and type **Jan**.

9. Use the fill handle of cell **B1** to create the series **Jan - Dec** in the range **B1:M1**.

10. Right align the range **B1:M1**, change the colour of the text to **Red** and the font to **Times New Roman**.

11. Click back in cell **A1** and on the **Developer** tab, in the **Code** group, click the **Stop Recording** button.

12. Save the workbook as an **Excel Macro-Enabled Workbook (*.xlsm)** with the name **Macros**.

13. Leave the workbook open.

i *The only way to amend a macro, without directly editing the **Visual Basic** code, is to record the whole sequence again.*

Driving Lesson 80 - Running a Macro

Park and Read

The macro can be activated in a variety of ways, depending on how it was set up. Some of the possible methods are covered in this Driving Lesson and the next one. Macros can be run:

> By listing the Macros and selecting from the list.
>
> By using a key press assigned to it.
>
> Adding it to the **Quick Access Toolbar** as a button and clicking on it.
>
> Assigning it to an object such as a box or a button on a sheet and clicking on it.

Manoeuvres

1.   The workbook **Macros** should still be open. If not, open it.

2.   Display **Sheet2**, click on any cell and on the **Developer** tab, in the **Code** group, click **Macros**.

 *The key press <**Alt F8**> is an alternative to the above command.*

3.   The **Macros** are listed. Click on the name **Months** and click **Run**. The months of the year will be added to the worksheet, right aligned, in red, Times New Roman font.

4.   Move to another **Sheet3,** click on a cell in the centre of the screen and press <**Ctrl m**>. This is the shortcut key press that was assigned to this macro when it was created in the previous Driving Lesson.

 Two different ways to run a macro are described in this Driving Lesson. How you choose to run a macro depends on the application and/or your personal preferences.

5.   Macros can easily be removed from a workbook. From any sheet display the **Macro** dialog boxes, click on the macro to remove, **Months** and click the **Delete** button.

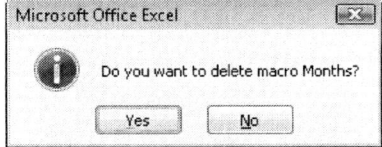

6.   Click **Yes** and the macro will be deleted.

7.   Close the workbook <u>without</u> saving.

Driving Lesson 81 - Assigning a Macro to the Quick Access Toolbar

 Park and Read

Macros can be added to buttons and placed on the **Quick Access Toolbar**, in any position. The Quick Access Toolbar is situated at the top left of the screen.

 Manoeuvres

1. Open the workbook **Hockey**, selecting **Enable Macros** when prompted. This has two macros attached to it.

2. Click the **Office** button, then **Excel Options** and display the **Customize** section.

 *The **Customize** section can be opened by using the drop down arrow at the right end of the **Quick Access Toolbar** and selecting **More Commands**.*

3. Select **Macros** from the **Choose commands from** box.

4. Click on the **Sort League** macro and click the **Add** button.

5. The macro is placed on the **Quick Access Toolbar**. The position can be changed by clicking on an item and using the up and down arrows on the right. Move the **Sort_League** macro up one place. Click **OK**.

6. Test the macro by clicking on the **Hockey.xlm!Sort_League** button, on the **Quick Access Toolbar**.

7. This is a macro specific to this workbook and therefore not appropriate for a toolbar button. To remove the button, display the **Customization** section, select the macro and click the **Remove** button. Click **OK**.

 *Macros attached to buttons are normally stored in the **Personal Macro Workbook** so that they work with all workbooks and are therefore applicable to any open workbook.*

8. Close the workbook <u>without</u> saving.

Driving Lesson 82 - S.A.E.

This is not an ECDL test. Testing may only be carried out through certified ECDL test centres. This is a Self-Assessment Exercise. Try to complete it without any reference to the Driving Lessons in this section.

1. Open the workbook **Macro Hotel**. This workbook contains the cash flow for a small hotel.

2. In cell **A2** enter your name.

3. A printout for each quarter is required. Create a macro to print the data for the first quarter (January to March), named **Q_one**. No quick key press and to work only in **This workbook**.

4. Run the macro **Q_one** to see if it works.

5. Create a similar macro for the second quarter (April to June), named **Q_two**.

6. Run the macro **Q_two** to see if it works.

7. Create a macro to change the orientation of the worksheet to landscape, name it **Landscape**.

8. Attach the macro to a button on the **Quick Access Toolbar** to the right of the **Save** button.

9. Change the orientation back to **Portrait** and preview the worksheet to check the number of pages and the orientation.

10. Try the macro button to see if works, check it using print preview.

11. Remove the **Macro Button** from the **Quick Access Toolbar**.

12. Delete the **Landscape** macro from the list of macros.

13. Close the workbook **Macro Hotel** <u>without</u> saving.

If you experienced any difficulty completing this S.A.E. refer back to the Driving Lessons in this section. Then redo the S.A.E.

Once you are confident with the features, complete the Record of Achievement Matrix referring to the section at the end of the guide. Only when competent move on to the next Section.

Section 17
Auditing

By the end of this Section you should be able to:

Use Auditing Tools

Trace Precedents and Dependents

Add and Remove Tracer Arrows

Trace Errors

To gain an understanding of the above features, work through the **Driving Lessons** in this **Section**.

For each **Driving Lesson**, read the **Park and Read** instructions, without touching the keyboard, then work through the numbered steps of the **Manoeuvres** on the computer. Complete the **S.A.E.** (Self-Assessment Exercise) at the end of the section to test your knowledge.

Driving Lesson 83 - Auditing

Park and Read

The **Auditing** features can be used to display the structure of calculations within a spreadsheet. They can be useful in helping to track down problems, particularly in complex worksheets with many formulas. The commands are available from the **Formulas** tab, **Formula Auditing** group.

Manoeuvres

1. Open the workbook **Audit Trail**. This contains some simple formulas so that auditing techniques can be demonstrated.

2. Display the **Formulas** tab.

3. The **Formula Auditing** group controls the functions associated with auditing.

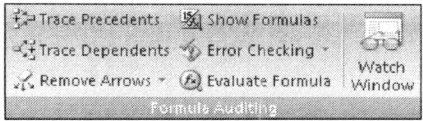

4. Place the cursor over each button in turn and check the **Tooltip**.

5. Click the drop down next to **Error Checking** to view the other commands.

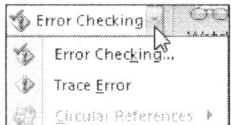

6. Click away from the menu to close it.

7. Leave the **Audit Trail** workbook open.

Driving Lesson 84 - Tracing Precedents

Park and Read

Precedents and **Dependents** are used to show the relationship between formulas and the cells that are used within them. **Precedents** are cells that are referenced by a formula in the current cell. Tracing precedents, looks at all the cells that have been used in the current formula.

Manoeuvres

1. The workbook **Audit Trail** should still be open. If not, open it. Display the **Sales** sheet.

2. To trace precedents for a formula, click the cell **E5** and then click the **Trace Precedents** button, `Trace Precedents`, in the **Formula Auditing** group.

	A	B	C	D	E	F
1						
2		Jan	Feb	Mar	Total	
3		13	6	4	23	
4		4	1	5	10	
5		17	7	9	33	
6						

The above diagram shows the Precedents for E5

3. With cell **E5** still selected, click the **Remove Arrows** drop down and select **Remove Precedent Arrows**. The arrow is removed.

4. **Precedents** can also be traced to other worksheets or workbooks. Select the **Accounts** sheet and click on cell **C4** (this references **E5** on the **Sales** sheet). Click the **Trace Precedents** button, .

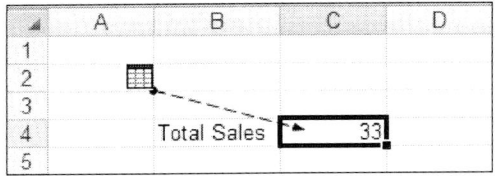

*The **Precedent** is traced to another sheet/book.*

5. To check where the link is from, double click anywhere on the arrow.

6. The **Go To** dialog box is displayed showing the source of formula. To go to the source, double click on the reference in the **Go to** box. It leads back to cell **E5** on the **Sales** sheet.

> *If the source is a different workbook it must be open, or an error is displayed.*

7. Leave the workbook **Audit Trail** open.

Driving Lesson 85 - Tracing Dependents

▣ Park and Read

Dependents are cells that reference the current cell. Tracing dependents looks at all other cells where the current cell is used in a formula.

☞ Manoeuvres

1. The workbook **Audit Trail** should still be open. If not, open it.

2. To trace **Dependents**, click on cell **C3** on the **Sales** sheet and click the **Trace Dependents** button, `Trace Dependents`.

	A	B	C	D	E
1					
2			Jan	Feb	Mar	Total
3			13	6	4	23
4			4	1	5	10
5			17	7	9	33
6					

The above diagram shows the dependents for C3, namely cells C5 and E3

3. With cell **C3** still selected, click the **Remove Arrows** drop down and select **Remove Dependent Arrows**.

4. To trace **Dependents** to other worksheets or workbooks, select cell **E5** and click the **Trace Dependents** button.

	A	B	C	D	E	F
1						
2		Jan	Feb	Mar	Total	
3		13		4	23	
4		4	1	5	10	
5		17	7	9	33	
6						

5. Cell **E5** is traced back to a linked worksheet/workbook. To check where the link is to, double click anywhere on the arrow.

6. The **Go To** dialog box is displayed showing the linked destination. Double click on the reference in the **Go to** box to go to the destination.

ℹ️ *If the destination is a different workbook it must be open, or a reference error is displayed.*

7. Leave the workbook **Audit Trail** open.

Driving Lesson 86 - Tracing Errors

▣ Park and Read

Auditing tools can be used to trace an error back to the source cell/s that cause the error. Tracing errors is similar to tracing precedents, but should only be used on cells that show an error value.

🕅 Manoeuvres

1. The workbook **Audit Trail** should still be open. If not, open it.

2. Display the **Accounts** sheet. Cells that contain errors are displayed with a # symbol. Select cell **E11** and click the **Error Checking** drop down, from the **Formula Auditing** group on the **Formulas** tab. Select **Trace Error**.

9	Sales Analysis				
10		Sales Achieved	Target Sales		Performance %
11		33		⬦	#DIV/0!
12					

ℹ️ *Selecting this option with the active cell not containing an error, results in an error message being displayed. A **Smart Tag** is displayed, ⬦, next to the cell containing the error.*

3. Double click the arrow to highlight the cell causing the error. Cell **C11** is made active. The error in **E11** is the result of the **Target Sales** cell not being completed.

4. **Comments** can be attached to cells that need an explanation of the contents. On the **Review** tab, click the **New Comment** button. Enter the comment **Do not leave this cell blank**.

5. Enter **40** in cell **C11**.

6. To remove all tracer arrows, on the **Formulas** tab, click the **Remove Arrows** button, ⟨ Remove Arrows ▾⟩. All the **Tracer Arrows** on the active worksheet are removed.

7. Leave the workbook **Audit Trail** open.

Driving Lesson 87 - S.A.E.

This is not an ECDL test. Testing may only be carried out through certified ECDL test centres. This is a Self-Assessment Exercise. Try to complete it without any reference to the Driving Lessons in this section.

1.   The workbook **Audit Trail** should still be open. If not, open it.

2.   Display the **Validation** sheet.

3.   Enter a new invoice on row **14**. Invoice number **178**, invoice date **today** in column **D**, drop the list down for the **Company** and choose **Spalding & Co** and the amount £**750**.

> **i** *The other three entries are all calculated from data entered. A **Validation List** has been added to **Column D** (validation is not part of this syllabus) and **Column C** uses a lookup table.*

4.   Trace the **Precedents** of cell **G8**.

5.   Trace the **Dependents** of cell **E11**.

6.   Trace the **Precedents** of cell **C13**. This used the company name in **Column D** and looks up the company number from the lookup table, **N5:O13**.

7.   Remove the **Precedent Arrows** from cell **C13**.

8.   Add your name in cell **D1**.

9.   Print a copy of the range **A1:G25**.

10.   Remove all the tracer arrows.

11.   Save the workbook as **Auditing**.

12.   Close the workbook.

> **i** *Check the answers at the back of the guide.*

If you experienced any difficulty completing this S.A.E. refer back to the Driving Lessons in this section. Then redo the S.A.E.

Once you are confident with the features, complete the Record of Achievement Matrix referring to the section at the end of the guide. Only when competent move on to the next Section.

Section 18
Shared Workbooks

By the end of this Section you should be able to:

Share Workbooks

Merge Workbooks

To gain an understanding of the above features, work through the **Driving Lessons** in this **Section**.

For each **Driving Lesson**, read the **Park and Read** instructions, without touching the keyboard, then work through the numbered steps of the **Manoeuvres** on the computer. Complete the **S.A.E.** (Self-Assessment Exercise) at the end of the section to test your knowledge.

Driving Lesson 88 - Shared Workbooks

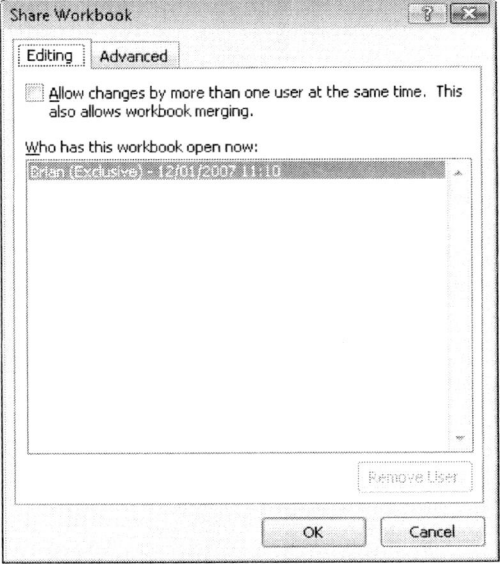 Park and Read

Sharing workbooks is a way of allowing different users to update the same spreadsheet. There are two ways of doing this. The spreadsheet can be updated by different users at the same time and all the changes will be updated whenever the file is saved, or at regular intervals.

Alternatively, copies of the shared spreadsheet can be sent out to different users. Each user updates their copy then returns it. The returned copies can then be merged together, with all the changes being either accepted or ignored.

Manoeuvres

1. Open the supplied workbook **Hotel**. This workbook is to be shared. Save the workbook as **Communal**.

2. To allow the workbook to be shared, on the **Review** tab, in the **Changes** group, click **Share Workbook**.

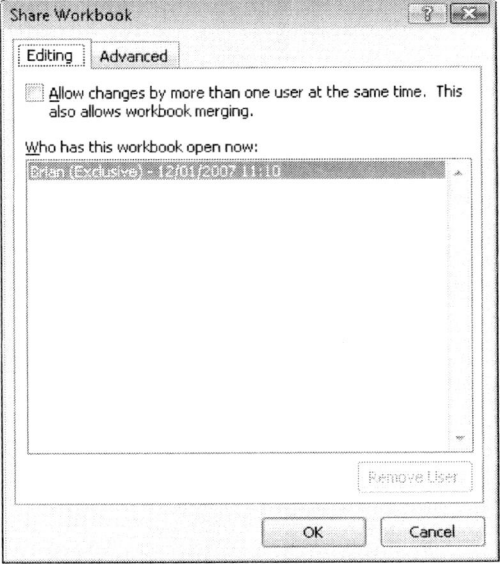

Driving Lesson 88 - Continued

3.   Click in the **Allow changes** option box, to activate it. Click the **Advanced** tab to see the available settings.

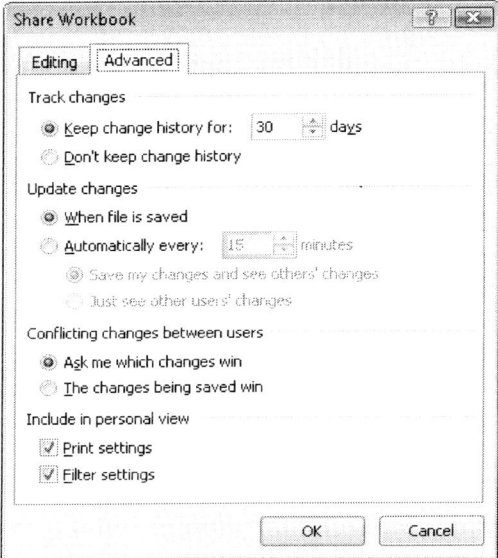

4.   Click **OK**. *Excel* will need to save the workbook with its new status and a message is displayed.

5.   Click **OK**. The workbook is saved as shared, and the title bar of the window will now show the word **Shared** next to the file name.

6.   If the file is saved in an accessible location, e.g. on a server, any other user can now open and amend any part of the file (unless it is protected) while it is still open on your computer.

Driving Lesson 88 - Continued

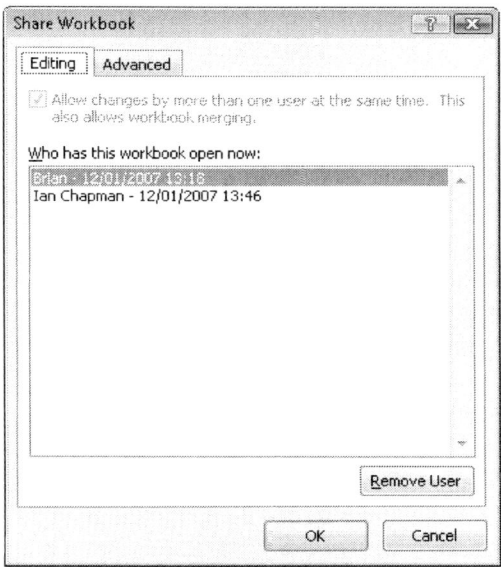

Some features cannot be applied or amended by anyone once a workbook is shared, e.g. charts, pictures, macros, hyperlinks, subtotals, scenarios, data tables, pivot tables and data validation.

7. To see who has a shared file open, select **Share Workbook** on the **Review** tab.

8. When another user changes data in the workbook, you will be notified and see the updates when you save your copy.

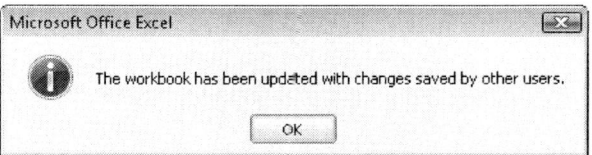

If you have both changed the same cell a dialog box will show both changes and give the option of accepting one or the other.

*By changing settings in the **Advanced** view of the **Share Workbook** dialog box, the updates can be applied automatically and regularly.*

9. Close the workbook **Communal**.

Driving Lesson 89 - Merging Workbooks

 Park and Read

Another way to share workbooks is to send copies out to various users so they can make their own amendments. The copies can then be merged back together, with the original user deciding which amendments to accept or ignore.

 Manoeuvres

1. Open the supplied workbook **Flights** and then save it as **Flights1**. This workbook is to be sent out for review but first it must be shared.

2. Select **Share Workbook** on the **Review** tab and click in the **Allow changes** option box in the **Editing** view.

3. Click the **Advanced** tab and change the history to 14 days. This means changes can be kept for up to 14 days and still be merged.

4. Click **OK** to share the workbook and **OK** again. Now the workbook can be sent out.

5. One way to send out the file is to email it. Click the **Office** button then **Send** and finally **Email**. Your mail application will open with the workbook attached ready to send, add the message **Please review the attached workbook**.

6. Address the message to another user and send it.

 Any method of sending out the workbook can be used, such as copying over a network or writing to a floppy disk or CD.

7. Open the workbook at its destination and make some small changes, e.g. change the value in cell **G2** from **4** to **2**.

8. Save the amended workbook with a different name, e.g. **Flights2**, and send it back to its original user. Make sure it is saved in the same location as the original, **Flights1**.

 *The **Compare and Merge Workbooks** command is not displayed by default in Excel 2007. To add it to the **Quick Access** toolbar, right click on the **Office** button and select **Customize Quick Access Toolbar** from the options. From the **Choose commands from** list select **All Commands**. From the list of commands in the category, select **Compare and Merge Workbooks**, click **Add**, and then **OK**.*

Driving Lesson 89 - Continued

9.   With the original **Flights1** file open, select **Compare and Merge Workbooks**, 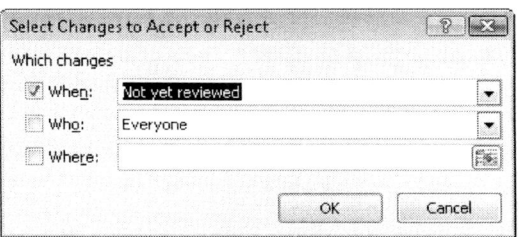, from the **Quick Access** toolbar.

10. Select the returned file (**Flights2**) from the **Select Files** dialog box and click **OK**.

11. To review the changes, display the **Review** tab and click **Track Changes** then **Accept/Reject Changes**.

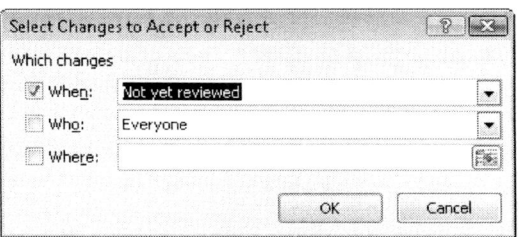

12. Leave the settings as shown and click **OK**. A dialog box will appear for each change in turn.

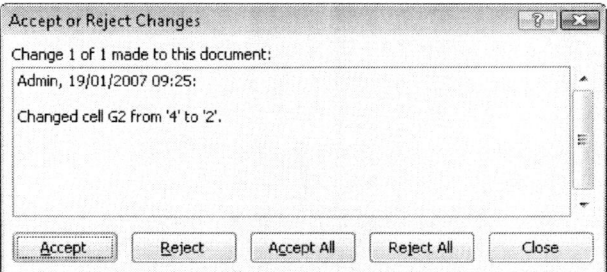

13. Each change can be accepted or rejected. If rejected, the original value will remain. Click **Accept**. When there are no more dialog boxes, all changes have been reviewed.

14. To remove the workbook from shared use, on the **Review** tab, click **Share Workbook**.

15. Uncheck the **Allow changes** option and click **OK**. Click **Yes** at the confirmation prompt.

16. Close the workbook **Flights1**.

Driving Lesson 90 - S.A.E.

This is not an ECDL test. Testing may only be carried out through certified ECDL test centres. This is a Self-Assessment Exercise. Try to complete it without any reference to the Driving Lessons in this section.

1.   Open the workbook **Draft**. As the managing director of the company, you want to allow your factory manager to amend the budget predictions you have created.

2.   Save the workbook as **Draft1**.

3.   Set the workbook up so that it can be amended by other users while you still have it open.

 For the benefit of people without network facilities, the updates in this exercise will actually be made <u>without</u> sharing.

4.   Set the workbook up to **Track changes while editing**.

5.   Save the workbook and close it.

6.   Now take the part of the factory manager. Open the **Draft1** workbook.

7.   You need extra workers in the summer to cover for holidays. Change the **Workers** value for **June**, **July** and **August** to **25**.

8.   The canteen roof is leaking. Insert a new row above **Overheads**. Enter a label of **Repairs** and a value of **£4000** in **January**.

9.   Change the **Overheads** figure for **April** to **£6000** to cover the annual golf competition. Save the workbook and close it.

10. Now you are the MD again. Open the **Draft1** workbook to review your manager's changes. Make sure the **Track Changes** option is set to track ALL changes.

11. Start the **Accept or Reject Changes** process. According to the dialog box, how many changes have been made?

12. Work through the changes, accepting the extra worker details and the overheads for the golf, but rejecting the repairs to the canteen (reject the insertion of the new row, and all associated changes will be lost).

13. You are feeling generous; add **£20** to the **Overheads** figure in **January** to buy new buckets for the canteen. What is the final **Total Net Profit** figure?

14. Remove the workbook from shared use, save it as **Draft1** and close it.

 Check the answers at the back of the guide.

If you experienced any difficulty completing this S.A.E. refer back to the Driving Lessons in this section. Then redo the S.A.E.

Once you are confident with the features, complete the Record of Achievement Matrix referring to the section at the end of the guide.

Answers

Driving Lesson 4

Step 1   It is easier to manage, different people can perform different tasks, people working on one part will not have access to the rest.

Step 2   So that any scrolling will only be in one direction. This makes a spreadsheet, easier to use, easier to understand and easier to print.

Step 3   Protecting the contents of cells that do not need to be changed stops them from being deleted, even accidentally. Sensitive data can also be password protected to stop unwanted viewing.

Step 4   You may need to produce a user guide, or provide training or act as a help desk.

Step 5   **Lists** (prices, materials, customers, range of units). **Linking** (displaying prices on a calculation sheet - orders). **Formulas** and **Functions** (to perform any calculations). **Formatting** (easier to use, pleasant for customers to see, good clear printouts etc.). **Analysis** (sales figures, stock used, profit, turnover, accounts etc). **Charts** (to represent figures). Plus any other item from page 11, depending on how you approach the task.

Step 6   A **template** is a base spreadsheet with all formatting and calculations included ready for data to be added. They are used repetitively for consistency.

Step 7   A **macro** is a method performing repetitive tasks with one action.

Step 8   As a **chart**, either: on paper, as a web page on the Internet, on a slide for a presentation.

Step 9   A **link** displays data <u>from</u> another source, a **hyperlink** <u>goes</u> to another location.

Driving Lesson 23

Step 5   The sales figure for February is **£2,000**.

Step 6   The amount of Spending in April is **£12,720**.

Driving Lesson 32

Step 2   The IF statement entered into cell J4 should be =IF(H4=0,0,((H4-I4)/I4)). This should then be replicated down the column as far as cell J10. There are 4 cells in the workbook that contain incorrect ranges in functions: The correct range for the function in cell H8 is (C8:G8). The correct range for the function in cell H10 is (H4:H9). The correct range for the function in cell E10 is (E4:E9). The correct range for the function in cell D10 is (D4:D9).

Driving Lesson 43

Step 4   The formula to calculate % occupancy would be =rooms/300.

Step 8   The completed chart.

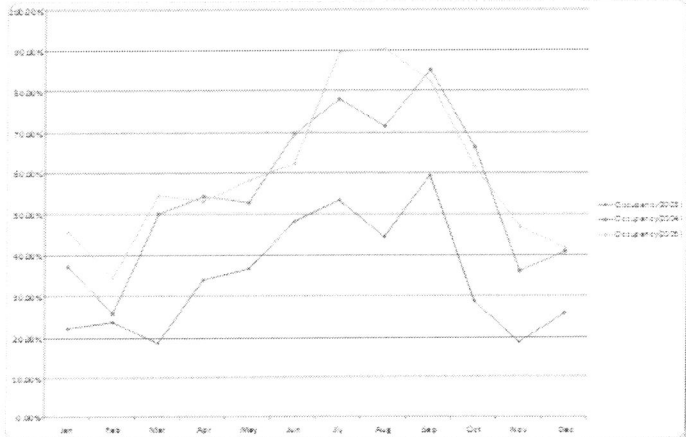

Driving Lesson 45

Step 16 The second cheapest car is the **Austin Mini**.

Step 17 The car with the most mileage is the **Fiat 126**.

Driving Lesson 56

Step 2   There are 3 members of staff in the Computer Services department.

Step 4   There are 7 members of staff aged between 40 and 50 years inclusive (remember that the ages are increasing continuously).

Step 8   3 records should have been extracted.

Driving Lesson 59

Step 3   The created Pivot Table.

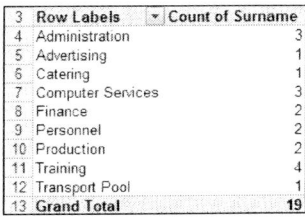

Step 8   The age group with the most absences is the **Over 50s**.

Driving Lesson 66

Step 12 The monthly repayment is £299.78

Step 13 The repayments rise to £366.88

Step 16 The maximum amount that can be borrowed is £40,885

Step 17 The result should be £447,107

Driving Lesson 67

Step 9   There should be a total of 75 replies

Step 10 The oldest person to reply is in their nineties

Step 11 The youngest person to reply is in their early twenties

Step 12 The total age of all respondents is more than 3300

Step 13 The average age of all respondents is over 44

Driving Lesson 68

Step 10 8 employees qualify for the bonus.

Driving Lesson 70

Answers for this type of exercise are continually changing due to the NOW() function and therefore are not provided.

Driving Lesson 77

Step 9   7 rooms

Step 11 Yes, profit of £20 rather than loss of £30.

Driving Lesson 87

Step 4   The Precedents of cell **G8** are cells **E8** and **F8**.

Step 5   The Dependents of cell **E11** are cells **F11** and **G11**.

Step 6   The Precedents of cell **C13** are cell **D13** and **N5**.

Driving Lesson 90

Step 11 **7** changes have been made

Step13   The total Net Profit is now **9108**

Glossary

Auditing
Allows relationships between formulas and their component cells/ranges to be displayed.

AutoFormat
Applies a set of pre-defined formatting to a worksheet in order to enhance its appearance.

AVERAGE
A function that adds the values in a range of cells, then divides the result by the number of values added.

Comment
Text that is attached to a cell as a background note. Displayed when the pointer is placed over the appropriate cell.

Concatenate
A function that can be used to combine the contents of two or more cells that contain text.

Container
A document that contains a link to a cell or range in a source document. If data in the source is modified, the container will automatically be updated.

COUNT
A function that will display the number of numerical values in a range of cells.

Data Table
Used to see how changing one variable in a formula affects its result.

Database Function
A function that is specifically designed to be used with lists.

Dependent
A cell that is referenced in a formula.

Delimited Text
Data within a text file, where the text is separated by commas, tabs, etc. This type of data may be imported into a worksheet.

Error
A message that is displayed when a formula cannot be calculated. The nature of the message identifies the reason for the error.

Field
A cell on a row within a list.

Field Name
The heading at the top of a column of fields within a list.

Filter
A tool that matches records in a list to specified criteria.

Formula
A calculation, can use values and/or cell references.

Freeze Panes
A command used to keep specific columns and/or rows on screen while scrolling through a worksheet.

Function
A specialised formula that makes calculations easier.

Go To
A command that can be used to navigate to a cell or range by using its reference or name.

Link   A formula reference to a cell or range in another location within the same worksheet, or another worksheet either in the same or a different workbook. A link allows data edited in the source worksheet to automatically update in the container worksheet. Links may be created to other file types.

List   A labelled series of rows that separates information into columns, each containing similar information.

Logical Function A function that tests the contents of a cell against a specified condition to see if it is true or false. Depending on the result, the function will perform one specified action or another.

Lookup   A function that looks up relevant data from a table, and uses it in a calculation.

Macro   A recorded sequence of commands that can be replayed as required in order to automate routine tasks.

Name   Cell or range references may be replaced by names to simplify navigation around a worksheet or understanding of formulae.

Nested Function A combination of individual functions combined with each other to perform more complex calculations.

PivotTable A table that organises and summarises large amounts of data from within a range of labelled columns. The fields within a PivotTable may be moved (Pivoted) around between the axes and data area to analyse the data in various ways.

Precedent A cell that is referenced by a formula.

Protection Passwords may be used to set various levels of security for cells, worksheets or workbooks

Record   A completed row of information within a list.

Scenario A specific combination of values and solutions that has been named and saved within a worksheet. This can then be compared to other combinations.

Source Document A worksheet containing data that is linked to a cell or range in a container worksheet. If this data is changed, the linked cell or range will automatically be updated.

SubTotal A function that can be applied to a list to display SUM, COUNT, or AVERAGE for each group with a grand total for the whole list.

SUM   A function that will add the values in a range of cells.

Summary Report A feature that lists all existing scenarios and displays an outline view of a selected scenario.

Template A base worksheet that provides a layout ready for data to be entered.

Index

Record of Achievement Matrix

This Matrix is to be used to measure your progress while working through the guide. This is a learning reinforcement process, you judge when you are competent.

Tick boxes are provided for each feature. 1 is for no knowledge, 2 some knowledge and 3 is for competent. A section is only complete when column 3 is completed for all parts of the section.

This is not an ECDL/ICDL test. Testing may only be carried out through certified ECDL/ICDL test centres.

Tick the Relevant Boxes **1**: No Knowledge   **2**: Some Knowledge   **3**: Competent

Section	No	Driving Lesson	1	2	3
1 Introduction	1	Spreadsheet Design			
	2	Techniques to Use			
	3	Using Hyperlinks in Excel			
2 Formatting	5	Freezing Titles			
	6	Conditional Formatting			
	7	Format As Table			
	8	Paste Special			
3 Protection	10	Protection			
	11	Worksheet and Cell Protection			
	12	Hiding Rows and Columns			
	13	Workbook Protection			
	114	Hiding Worksheets and Workbooks			
4 Cell Comments	16	Cell Comments			
	17	Display Comments			
	18	Create, Edit & Delete Comments			
5 Names	20	Names			
	21	Using Names in Formulas			
	22	Using Go To with Names			
6 Templates	24	Creating a Template			
	25	Using a Template			
	26	Editing a Template			
	27	Deleting a Template			
7 Formulas	29	Displaying Formulas			
	30	Formulas that Produce Errors			
	31	Custom Number Formats			
8 Scenarios	33	Creating Scenarios			
	34	Using and Editing Scenarios			
	35	Scenario Summary Reports			

Tick the Relevant Boxes **1**: No Knowledge   **2**: Some Knowledge   **3**: Competent

Section	No	Driving Lesson	1	2	3
9 Linking & Importing	37	Linking			
	38	Creating Links			
	39	Linking between Workbooks			
	40	Linking to a Word Document			
	41	Exporting Data			
	42	Importing Data			
10 Sorting	44	Sorting			
	45	Multiple Column Sorts			
	46	Custom Sorts			
11 Lists	48	Lists			
	49	Creating a List			
	50	Filtering Lists			
	51	AutoFilter			
	52	Custom AutoFilter			
	53	Advanced Filtering			
	54	Extracting Filtered Data			
	55	Adding Sub Totals			
12 Pivot Tables	57	Pivot Tables			
	58	Grouping Data in PivotTables			
13 Functions	60	Functions			
	61	Logical Functions			
	62	Date and Time Functions			
	63	Lookup Functions			
	64	Maths & Statistical Functions			
	65	Text Functions			
	66	Financial Functions			
	67	Database Functions			
	68	Nested Functions			
	69	Trends			

Tick the Relevant Boxes **1**: No Knowledge   **2**: Some Knowledge   **3**: Competent

Section	No	Driving Lesson	1	2	3
14 Charts	71	Formatting Charts			
	72	Modifying Charts			
	73	Insert Image in 2D Chart			
15 Data Tables	75	One Input Data Table			
	76	Two Input Data Table			
16 Macros	78	Macros			
	79	Recording a Macro			
	80	Running a Macro			
	81	Assigning a Macro to the Quick Access Toolbar			
17 Auditing	83	Auditing			
	84	Tracing Precedents			
	85	Tracing Dependents			
	86	Tracing Errors			
18 Shared Workbooks	88	Shared Workbooks			
	89	Merging Workbooks			

Other Products from CiA Training

CiA Training is a leading publishing company, which has consistently delivered the highest quality products since 1985. A wide range of flexible and easy to use self teach resources has been developed by CiA's experienced publishing team to aid the learning process. These include the following materials at the time of publication of this product:

- **ECDL/ICDL Syllabus 4.0 (ECDL Foundation Qualification)**
  - o **Module 1 - Concepts of Information Technology (IT)**
  - o **Module 2 - Using the Computer and Managing Files**
  - o **Module 3 - Word Processing**
  - o **Module 4 - Spreadsheets**
  - o **Module 5 - Database**
  - o **Module 6 - Presentation**
  - o **Module 7 - Information and Communication**
- **ECDL/ICDL Advanced (ECDL Foundation Qualification)**
  - o **Advanced Module AM3 Word Processing**
  - o **Advanced Module AM4 Spreadsheets**
  - o **Advanced Module AM5 Database**
  - o **Advanced Module AM6 Presentation**
- **Revision Books (Support Materials for ECDL/ICDL Qualifications)**
  - o **Syllabus 4 (All 7 modules in a single book)**
  - o **Advanced AM3 Word Processing**
  - o **Advanced AM4 Spreadsheets**
  - o **Advanced AM5 Database**
  - o **Advanced AM6 Presentation**
- **e-Citizen Book (ECDL Foundation Qualification)**

We hope you have enjoyed using our materials and would love to hear your opinions about them. If you'd like to give us some feedback, please go to:

www.ciatraining.co.uk/feedback.php

and let us know what you think.

New products are constantly being developed. For up to the minute information on our products, to view our full range, to find out more, or to be added to our mailing list, visit:

www.ciatraining.co.uk